# The Stable Society

*Its Structure and Control*

Towards a Social Cybernetics

by
**Edward Goldsmith**

The Wadebridge Press, 73 Molesworth Street,
Wadebridge, Cornwall, England

*First published in 1978
by The Wadebridge Press
73 Molesworth Street, Wadebridge,
Cornwall, England*


*Printed in Great Britain
by Penwell Ltd., Parkwood, Dupath,
Callington, Cornwall.*

*Hardback: ISBN 0 9504111 3 2
Paperback: ISBN 0 9504111 4 0*

# CONTENTS

Continued.

**4**  Science and Social Control  53

*The attempt to substitute apparently object-
ive knowledge for the subjective knowledge
contained in a society's religio-culture, in
order to enable it to adapt to more improbable
environmental situations, violates basic
cybernetic principles and can only lead to
social disintegration, increased instability
and eventual collapse.*

## APPENDICES

# Introduction

Our society is increasingly unstable. It is subject to increasing discontinuities which, if unchecked, must lead it to eventual collapse. More and
more people are realising this. More and more, too, are aware of the
necessity for creating a steady-state or a stable society, one whose
activities do not lead to the systematic destruction of its natural
environment.

Not surprisingly, many students of these matters have considered what
must be some of the characteristics of such a society. Their interest,
however, has been largely monopolised by its economic and demographic
characteristics. Population growth and economic activities, however, are
but two aspects of a society's total behaviour pattern. What is more, their
nature is influenced, indeed largely determined, by the other aspects that
are often unknown to demographers and economists. Only a society with a
particular structure and world view is likely to be capable of controlling its
relationship with its environment so as to avoid the sort of discontinuities
to which ours is increasingly subject.

In this book, which consists of four papers that have already appeared
separately in different journals, I try to determine what are the structural
and cognitive characteristics of a stable society.

It is not difficult to show to what extent a science-based modern society
fails to satisfy these conditions. On the other hand, a tribal society can be
examined in the light of Cybernetics and General-Systems Theory in
that its behaviour can be described in terms of the same set of variables
required to describe the behaviour of other natural systems such as a
biological organism or a non-human society.

The strategies exploited by tribal societies to maintain their stable
relationship with their environment are then examined, as is the way they
must break down as a tribe under the influence of development disintegrating into a modern mass society.

The lesson of this book is that we cannot postulate utopian socio-
economic forms without reference to those that man has been able to
develop in the past, the basic features of which must be present in any
society that does not violate what must be regarded as the basic laws

governing the behaviour of stable and hence, in the long term, viable social systems.

To try to do so would be very much like trying to invent an alternative biology without reference to biological theory or to the biological forms that evolution has brought into being.

## Acknowledgments

Much of the material in this book has been derived from the 'Theory of Unified Science' an unpublished manuscript that I finished in 1967. The first chapter is based on an article that appeared in *The Ecologist* in January 1976, and the second chapter on a paper read at the International Cultural Foundation's Fourth International Conference on the Unity of the Sciences held in New York in 1975, and that also appeared in *The Ecologist* in February 1976. The third chapter was published in very shortened form in *The Ecologist* in November 1974 and the fourth chapter is based on a paper read at the Third International Conference on the Unity of the Sciences held in London in 1974 and then appeared in *The Ecologist* in February 1975. I must thank Jimoh Omo Fadaka for his article, 'The Family Basis of Social Structure in Benin' (Appendix VI), written to show how the structure of his society can be understood in terms of the model proposed in this book. It was also published in *The Ecologist* in July 1976. Thanks are also due to Bernard Gilbert and Brenda Duxbury for helping me organise the material and preparing it for publication.

# 1 Society as a Natural System

Governments throughout the World are failing dismally to solve the problems that confront them, and to control the societies that have elected them to office. There are many reasons: one, however, is that we have overestimated the powers of legislation to solve biological, social and ecological problems. Over a thousand years ago, King Canute demonstrated to his courtiers just what were the limits to legislation. He pointed out that the waves, like the other forces of nature, were indifferent to his exhortations, and that their movement could not be controlled by government edicts.

The organisation of human and non-human societies is determined by natural forces, which, like those that determine the structure of all other natural systems, obey a very precise set of laws. Although governments may try to command these forces, they will succeed only to the extent that they observe Hobbes's dictum: "We cannot command nature, except by obeying her."

The very secondary role which institutions play in determining the course of history has been pointed out by the few really profound political thinkers of the nineteenth century, who, in the age of superficiality in which we live, are scarcely remembered, and still more rarely studied.

Edward Hartpole Lecky wrote:[1] "It is a great error, both in history and in practical politics, to attach too much value to a political machine. The essential consideration is by what men and in what spirit that machine is likely to be worked. Few Constitutions contain more theoretical anomalies, and even absurdities, than that under which England has attained to such an unexampled height of political prosperity; while a servile imitation of some of the most skilfully-devised Constitutions in Europe has not saved some of the South American States from long courses of anarchy, bankruptcy and revolution."

This is also Buckle's view of institutional controls.[2] "It is not by the wax and parchment of lawyers," he wrote, "that the independence of men can be preserved. Such things are the mere externals; they set off liberty to advantage; they are as its dress and paraphernalia, its holiday-suit in

1

times of peace and quiet. But, when the evil days set in, when the invasions of despotism have begun, liberty will be retained, not by those who can show the oldest deed and the largest charters, but by those who have been most inured to habits of independence, most accustomed to think and act for themselves, and most regardless of that insidious protection which the upper classes have always been so ready to bestow, that, in many countries, they have now left nothing worth the trouble to protect.''

What then is the role of institutions? Their only useful role, according to Gustave le Bon,[3] is to provide a legal sanction for changes which customs and public opinion have come to accept. *They follow such changes but do not precede them.* It is not by means of institutions that one can modify the character and the thought of men. Nor is it by means of institutions that a people can be rendered religious or sceptical, or taught to govern itself instead of calling without cease upon the State to enslave it.''

Unfortunately, with us, the study of societies is very much that of their institutions. If one society is more successful than another, we attribute its success to the specific institutions by which it is governed. If it fails, then the failure is automatically regarded as an institutional one. It does not occur to us *that the society itself might be at fault* — that certain societies in fact, such as the industrial nation-states of today, have become quite uncontrollable, regardless of the subtlety of their institutions or of the genius of those who manipulate them.

Our ignorance of social realities is also largely attributable to our tendency to concentrate on modern societies. The notion that the social experience of Paleolithic man, for instance, may be relevant to our own is rarely considered, in spite of the fact that probably more than 90 per cent of all the men who have ever lived did so during the Paleolithic period. To suppose that we are exempted from the laws which governed their behaviour by virtue of our familiarity with science and technology is but an act of faith — one which serves to rationalise the systematic and ever more radical violation of these laws by the industrial activities to which our society is committed.

If we overcome our presumption and examine the social life of Paleolithic, indeed of tribal man in general, we discover that, underlying the impressive variety of cultural forms which still monopolises the attention of anthropologists, there are fundamental similarities.*

One common denominator of tribal societies is the relative absence

---

* Real science begins when interest shifts from the accumulation of trivia so as to determine in what minute ways things differ from each other, to the study of what they have in common. In this way 'data' are organised to constitute 'information' which can be of use for influencing policy.

among them of governmental institutions. "It should be noted," Lowie writes on this subject,[4] "that the legislative function in most primitive countries seems strangely curtailed when compared with that exercised in the more complex civilizations. All the exigencies of normal social intercourse are covered by customary law, and the business of such governmental machinery as exists is rather to exact obedience to traditional usage than to create new precedents."

Indeed, in pre-agricultural societies, nothing can be found to correspond to our notion of government. There are rarely kings, or even chiefs, no presidents or courts of law, no prisons or police force. The closest approximation to a political institution is the council of elders which occasionally gathers to discuss important issues. Such a society has often been referred to as a 'gerontocracy', or a government by the old men — a term that can be applied to most stable societies. It might be more apt, however, to speak of a 'necrocracy', or government by the dead, since, as Lowie points out, the role of the elders is simply to interpret the traditions and customary laws of the tribe, which embody the experience and practices of previous generations.

A society of this sort usually displays a very high degree of order. The absence of formal institutions, rather than giving rise to the permissiveness that we would expect, is in fact associated with firm discipline and the strictest possible adherence to the tribal code of ethics. Behaviour which, in a disordered society, could only be exacted at the cost of brutal coercion, is, in a tribal society, assured via the agency of public opinion, the sanction of the elders, and the fear of incurring the displeasure of the ancestral spirits.[5] The great discipline displayed by traditional societies in general is the main theme of Fustel de Coulanges in his famous book, *La Cité Antique.*[6]

Where public opinion is effective, there is correspondingly little need for governmental institutions for maintaining order. Conversely societies in which public opinion is weak require the most authoritarian government linked to an all-pervasive and coercive bureaucracy to maintain a semblance of public order, in the absence of which there can be but lawlessness and mob-rule.

The notion that effective democracy could be introduced into a society by the simple expedient of adopting the correct institutions is a sad illusion, and one, unfortunately, that we seem very reluctant to shed.

### Societies and Organisms
If modern man is convinced that he has nothing to learn from the study of tribal societies, he is even more convinced of the irrelevance to his problems of the social experience of non-human animals. To justify this

particular act of faith, appeal is made to a host of undefined faculties whose possession is supposed to differentiate man as radically as possible from all other forms of life (see Appendix I).

The truth is that the difference between non-human animal societies and human animal societies is one of degree rather than of kind; in the former culturally determined behaviour plays a much bigger role than in the latter, and in reality the behaviour of both societies can be understood in terms of of the same model using the same set of variables.

It has also been observed by biologists, ecologists and sociologists that there are marked functional similarities between a society (whether human or non-human) and an organism.

Maeterlinck[7] described the extraordinary similarity between a termite colony and an organism. "There is perhaps no other solution," he writes, "than to consider a termite colony as an individual."

Tinbergen[8] regards a society as a sort of super-organism. "The main difference," he writes, "between individual and community is one of level of integration; in a community integration has been carried one step beyond the individual."* With the growing realisation that the functional similarities between societies and organisms extend also to many other forms of natural and social organisation, there have developed the associated fields of cybernetics and general systems. In terms of these essential, unifying theories, the society and the organism are not only related to each other, but are seen as specialised instances of something much more general — of what has come to be called *a system* (or, to distinguish it from the system referred to by engineers, *a natural system*).

---

* Here in full is the comparison Tinbergen makes. "When studying the way in which a community is organised," he writes, "one is often struck by the many parallels that can be drawn between it and an individual. Both are composed of constituent parts; the individual is composed of organs, the community of individuals. In both, there is division of labour between the component parts. In both, the parts cooperate for the benefit of the whole, through it for their own benefit. The constituent partners give and receive. Thus they lose part of their 'sovereignty' as well as part of their capacity to lead a life in isolation. The loss of sovereignty can go so far that parts give their own life for the benefit of the whole. There is constant loss of skin cells in the individual; a lizard's tail is left for the predator for the benefit of the rest of the lizard, so that this rest can live and reproduce. A mother duck defends her chicks even at the cost of her own life. The benefits that the parts derive from the whole is obvious in the individual; an isolated muscle cannot live long. But neither can an isolated worker of the honey bee nor an isolated polyp of a Siphonophore colony. Even in cases where individuals can live in isolation, they lose the manifold benefits they receive when living in the flock . . . Loss of capacity to live outside the community is more striking in the organs of an individual which has derived its name from it; yet the difference is one of degree only. There are individuals which can very well be divided into parts without fatal consequences; tape worms, Planarias and sea anemones are not 'undividable'. Comparison of individual and community leading to the idea of the community as a 'super-organism' is of great use to the sociologist. Of course it must not be carried too far; organism and community cannot be identified; yet it helps one to realise that in both cases one has to do with a 'going concern', presenting problems of organisation and cooperation. The main difference between individual and community is one of level of integration, in a community integration has been carried one step beyond the individual."

## Society as a System

A system is considered to be made up of differentiated parts in dynamic interrelationship with each other.

I prefer to regard a system however, as a unit of behaviour,* for if this behaviour is to be self regulating and adaptive, the entity that is behaving must be so constituted. Needless to say, it has not occurred to most sociologists today that a society can be considered in this light. The main reason is that their attention has been monopolised by modern societies which are no longer capable of self regulation nor of adaptation to their environment and which have long ago lost their basic structure.

Modern societies are in fact disintegrated systems. Primitive tribal societies however can be shown to observe the basic laws that govern the behaviour of all other natural systems, i.e. their behaviour is explicable in terms of basic cybernetic and general systems theory. It is not surprising that we have failed to understand that a society is a natural system since we have not yet understood that a family is one either. Indeed, many people still insist on regarding the family as an outdated relic of our barbaric past that should be replaced by some more up-to-date grouping to be designed by modern social scientists. It is also worth noting that the notion of an 'ecosystem' is of very recent origin and that but a few decades ago we had not yet noticed that the discreet units into which nature could be divided (forests, lakes, marshes etc.) also constituted natural systems.

*It is difficult to overemphasise the implications of our refusal to accept that man is a part of larger systems such as a society, an ecosystem, and a family.* It is very much like cells failing to 'realise' that they are part of a biological organism. In both cases, it would be assumed that behaviour tended only to satisfy individual ends and was not subject to the constraints that would enable it to satisfy the requirements of the larger system which, being dependent for its very existence on the cooperation of its parts, would then be condemned to inevitable disintegration. In a biological organism, this development is referred to as cancer. The cells proliferate in a purely random manner, precisely as do the members of a modern urban society and the parts of an ecosystem that its industrial activities have devastated.

## Directivity

Let us now consider the main features of systems, and, more precisely,

---

* To constitute a unit of behaviour it must display order, which means that its parts must be differentiated and interrelated. It is this latter aspect of a system that has most attracted the attention of those involved in the study of general systems.[9]

One must be careful in distinguishing between behavioural systems and the man-made systems studied by engineers. As we shall see man-made systems do not display the basic features of natural systems as described in this paper.

those which we must take into account if we are to understand the nature and function of the family in the context of a general model of behaviour.

The first and most important principle is that they are goal-directed or directive[10] (see Appendix II). This follows from basic theoretical principles, and is the only hypothesis reconcilable with the available empirical data. What is more, it can be shown that cultural behaviour, i.e. the behaviour of social systems, is as directive as that of biological organisms (see Appendix III).

The extraordinary similarity of cultural forms throughout the world tends to confirm the directive character of cultural behaviour. Whereas the early ethnologists saw these similarities as the result of cultural diffusion, more recent theories attribute them to cultural 'convergence', in the sense that systems with similar potentialities have tended to adapt in a similar way to similar environmental situations (see Appendix IV).

## Stability

What is the goal? The answer is stability. This is not defined as a fixed point in space-time but as a course or trajectory along which discontinuities, i.e. disequilibria and their corrections, are reduced to a minimum, and which thereby ensures survival taken in its widest sense. Human societies until recently satisfied this requirement.[11] Their culturally determined goal was the maintenance of traditional norms, which were upheld by public opinion, the council of elders, and the ancestral spirits. Stability is another word for continuity. It does not mean immobility, as an immobile system, being unable to adapt to a changing environment, would not be stable. Once we have accepted that stability is the goal, we have at our disposal an objective criterion for judging behavioural strategies, including those exploited to control human societies. Instead of making arbitrary or subjective judgements, we can evaluate these strategies *in accordance with what can be the only objective criterion: the extent to which they contribute towards stability.*

Unfortunately, if one applies this criterion, it is impossible to justify the principal features of the industrial way of life, indeed of industrial society in general, which tends systematically in that direction which can only lead to increasing instability — hence, to ever more serious discontinuities, and eventual collapse.

## Self-Regulation

Stable systems must be self-regulating. They are maintained on their course by a control mechanism or 'cybernism' which, in all systems, regardless of their level of organisation, functions on the same principle. Data are detected, interpreted and 'cybernised' to constitute a model of the relationship of the system to its environment. In a social system this model is usually referred to as a world-view or *Weltanschauung*. The

6

responses are mediated in terms of it, otherwise they would be random from the point of view of the larger system (made up of the system functioning within its environment) which would thereby be out of control.

The gene[12] and the brain,[13] however dissimilar they may appear to the outside observer, are functionally the same. They are both 'cybernisms' or control-mechanisms, as is a gene-pool and also that association of brains in which is organised the world-view of a society. The gene controls the process of protein synthesis, in a manner that has now been established in some detail.*

The relationship between a gene and the corresponding process of protein synthesis is functionally that existing between any cybernism and the behavioural process that it mediates, for example, a society's world-view and what we may call 'sociosynthesis' — the process by which a society develops and is renewed with each successive generation. In each case, information organised in a cybernismic medium is transduced into that of a behavioural one. In other words, instructions are translated into action.

This first involves classifying the environment very precisely in terms of that 'particular language or alphabet' in which the information in the model is formulated. In the case of 'sociosynthesis', this alphabet, which, as we shall see, consists of kinship terms, serves to classify: a) all the members of the family; b) by extension, all those of the community, of the clan, and of all intermediary associations; c) the members of the pantheon, i.e. those members of the family, the community, the clan, etc.,

---

* The process of protein synthesis was first described by Quick, Griffiths and Orgel.[12] An enzyme is a very large protein molecule. It consists of hundreds of amino-acid units, arranged in a chain in a very specific order. The ordering of the amino-acid units must be determined by a corresponding set of instructions, which are now known to be transmitted by the genes. Beadle, experimenting with a very simple form of life, the fungus *Neurospora,* showed that the genes specify which enzymes are to be synthesised — each gene specifies a single enzyme.

How this is accomplished was eventually shown by Crick and Watson. It was revealed that the medium or language in terms of which information is organised in a gene makes use of an 'alphabet' of four different nucleotides. Information organised in the protein molecules, on the other hand, makes use of an 'alphabet' having twenty basic classifications (the twenty different types of amino-acid unit). Crick showed how information is transmitted from one medium to another. If the four basic nucleotides are grouped into triplets, the number of combinations produced is sufficient to code the twenty classifications used by the protein. Crick went on to show *how this transduction is achieved.* An RNA molecule containing the information of the gene is produced in the nucleus and travels into the cytoplasm to a ribosome, where it serves as a template or model for the synthesis of a protein. The amino-acids that are to be linked together to form the protein first attach themselves to a molecule of so-called transfer RNA synthesised in the cytoplasm. In this way each amino-acid molecule is given an identity that makes it recognisable to the template RNA. The transfer RNA links each amino-acid to its own specific triplet on the template RNA and, when the amino-acids are joined end-to-end, the enzyme has been manufactured.

who have died and become ancestors; d) the physical environment.

It is in this way and only in this way that *an individual can respond to his environment as a whole with a single integrated behaviour pattern based on a single integrated model of his total environment.*

## Generality

Behaviour proceeds from the general to the particular. In embryology this is referred to as Van Baer's second law. The earlier stages are the most important, as they will colour all subsequent ones. This means that errors in the earlier parts of any behavioural process are of far more consequence than those occurring in the later phases. This explains the tremendous importance of the family, which provides the correct environment for the earlier phases of the ontogenetic process. Maternal deprivation in all animals requiring parental tutelage and hence brought up within the family environment must in general give rise to subsequent problems of social maladjustment.[14]

## Differentiation

The reason why the generalities colour the particularities is that development occurs by differentiation and that the particularities of any behavioural pattern have been designed, by the developmental process involved, to assure the more adaptive implementation of strategies previously assured in a more general way. Thus, as we pass from the amoeba, whose single cell fulfils all those functions that are necessary to the maintenance of life, such as the seizing of prey, its digestion, the excretion of waste matter, respiration, reproduction, locomotion, etc., to the complex multi-cellular organism into which it eventually evolves, we find that the same functions are fulfilled but in an increasingly more differentiated manner.

In other words, there have developed specialised mechanisms that are increasingly well adapted for the performance of functions previously fulfilled in a more general way, originally by a single cell. The same is true, as we shall see, as the extended family evolves into a community.

## Order

As soon as systems associate to form a larger system, they are subjected to a new set of constraints. These do not replace the others but supplement them. Constraints, in fact, accumulate as systems advance up the ladder of life, as they move from one level of organisation to the next.

The actual strength of the constraints imposed upon a system is a measure of its order or negative-entropy — which terms are used synonymously. Order is usually defined in terms of limitation of choice, or what is the same thing, the influence of the whole over the parts.

A family displays order, and can thereby exist as a unit of behaviour or a system, because its members accept the constraints which membership of the family imposes on their behaviour. The acceptance of these constraints leads them to fulfil specific family functions to the exclusion of the others. They have thus become differentiated and hence interrelated parts of the social system. The greater the degree of differentiation, the greater their dependence on the other members of the family for the fulfilment of complementary functions. In this way, the influence of the whole over the parts is correspondingly increased, as is its order or negative-entropy.

## Homeotely and the Hierarchical Cooperation Principle

In an ordered system the parts cooperate with each other — their behaviour tends towards the same goal. Their behaviour may be described as 'homeotelic' (from the Greek *Homoeo* = same, and *telos* = goal). When a system breaks down and its parts tend towards different goals, their behaviour will be referred to as 'heterotelic' (from the Greek *hetero* = different). Why, one might ask, should the parts of a system cooperate, especially as this means accepting constraints on their behaviour? The answer is that by virtue of the Differentiation Principle they have been designed phylogenetically and ontogenetically to fulfil specific functions within a given environment (that constituted by the larger system of which they are the differentiated parts). When the parts of a system are fulfilling the functions for which they have been designed they are themselves best adjusted, and their needs are best satisfied (the implications of this situation for the environment are considered below in the Optimum Environment Principle).

The operation of this principle at the level of the family is quite evident. By behaving in a certain way towards her husband and children, a mother fulfils her normal functions and thereby ensures the survival of the family. She behaves in this way because *in so doing she best satisfies her own basic physical and psychological needs*. The Hierarchical Cooperation Principle can in fact be stated thus: in an ordered system, that behaviour which satisfies the needs of the differentiated parts will also satisfy the needs of the whole. As we shall see, this is undoubtedly so in a traditional tribal society. It is no longer so, unfortunately, in a modern state — hence the need for institutions and external controls in order to force people to behave contrary to their natural inclinations.

## Succession

Another principle of development which emerges from such an approach can be referred to as the Sequential Principle, or the Principle of

Succession as it is known in ecology. All behavioural processes are arranged to form a sequence of steps. These steps must occur in the right order. If one step in the sequence does not occur, the sequence can proceed no further. In addition, the environmental situations to which behavioural processes constitute adaptive reactions, and to which each of its steps is therefore linked, must also occur in exactly the right order.

Thus, if a given step does not occur at the 'right time', it will not occur at all, or at best but imperfectly. Once more, embryology furnishes us with a very clear illustration of this principle.

Discriminatory ability is low in an embryological system, where the cytoplasm constitutes a very highly ordered environment. In such a situation, environment 'A' triggers off reaction 'a', which in turn gives rise to a modified environment, 'B', which in turn triggers off specific reaction 'b', etc. It is evident that in these conditions any departure from the correct sequence of environmental situations and of behavioural reactions will prevent the total process from occurring.

Similarly, in the development of an ecosystem, or of the ecosphere as a whole, the steps must occur in the right order. The biosphere cannot support carnivores until it has first given rise to herbivores, and the latter cannot possibly come into being unless the requisite vegetation has first appeared. Only a fixed sequence of events, from which but slight deviations can be tolerated, can account for the development of the highly complex biosphere of which we are part.

This partly explains why social maladjustments resulting from family maladjustments in early life, in particular maternal deprivation, are in general untreatable by medical or institutional means.

### Continuity of Information
Systems must be looked at four-dimensionally. They exist in time as well as in space and their continuity can only be assured if the information transmitted from one generation to the next reflects the experience of the system as a whole, stretching as far back along its evolutionary history as is relevant to the conditions of the day.

We know that this is true of genetic information. That is why it appears so nonplastic — and why some scientists believe (wrongly) that it is not affected by environmental factors. What is not generally realised is that it has until recently been true also of cultural information. Education until recently consisted in imbuing youth with the traditional wisdom accumulated over many generations. In this way, the individual was led to adopt the world-view and the behaviour pattern which had proved most adaptive in the environmental conditions to which the society was subjected.

If these environmental conditions are modified too radically, the model is unlikely to represent the new situation adequately. The model must have a certain inertia. This inertia is adaptive, if the term is used correctly,[15] since to modify the model in such a way that it gives rise to a totally new behaviour pattern would mean transforming the system too radically. This would be self-defeating, since it would entail a loss of continuity or stability, and, as we have seen, *to maintain the system's continuity is precisely the goal of behaviour*. In any case the system could not survive if the model on which its behaviour pattern was based represented a short-term or freak situation that probably would never recur.

This is an essential point, although there is a general failure to appreciate it among the adepts of 'progress', who tend to be ignorant of the very principles by which information is organised and transmitted within natural systems. Significantly, systems can only classify things in terms of the classifications that have proved useful in interpreting their relationship to the environment to which they have so far been submitted. Thus, the Tahitians,[16] when they first saw horses, classified them as 'man-carrying pigs', because the pig was the only quadruped of which they had any experience. If a rhinoceros were put in a shoe-factory, it could only classify the machines, the piles of shoes, and all the other constituents of this new and strange environment in a way relevant to its personal experience and that of its species. Because our industrial society is so far removed from that in which we evolved phylogenetically, our own situation is increasingly like that of the rhinoceros in the shoe factory.

It may be useful to coin the term 'cognitive maladjustment' to refer to this situation.* This is what Forrester speaks of as the 'counterintuitivity' of our social environment, which he wrongly attributes to its growing complexity.[17]

**The Optimum Environment**
From what we have said, it follows that one can only understand the behaviour of a system by examining it in its optimum environment, that to which it has been adapted phylogenetically and ontogenetically. To examine it in an artificial environment is only useful in order to understand the resulting behavioural aberrations. Zuckerman[18] made this mistake, when he assumed that the baboons in the London Zoo which he studied were typical baboons rather than very untypical ones living in the totally artificial conditions of captivity.

It is significant that for well over 90 per cent of man's tenancy of this planet he has earned his living by hunting and gathering, and his

* See also Chapter 4 'Science and Social Control'.

activities have been limited to the fulfilment of his normal ecological functions in his natural environment, i.e., he has until extremely recently behaved as a normal differentiated part of the biosphere. When we generalise about man, we should consequently be referring implicitly to 'man the hunter'.[19] Man's experience as an industrialist is not more than the equivalent of two days in the life of a man of 70, in fact quite negligible; *it is certainly far too short a sample on which to base any generalisations about the behaviour of man.* If one talks of man in general, one must thereby be referring to man the hunter.

It must follow that sociologists who only study man in the urban setting of today are making exactly the mistake that Zuckerman made when studying baboons in the London Zoo.

### The Geneto-Cultural Continuum
The behaviour pattern of a natural system constitutes an integrated whole, not just an unrelated or random patchwork of expedients. We have seen above what are its organisational principles. This must be as true of the behaviour of a social system as of that of an organism (see Appendix V). For this to be so, such behaviour must be based on a single organisation of information or model of a system's relationship to its environment. This has important implications which neither those involved in the so-called natural sciences nor those in the social sciences have been willing to face. The behaviour of an advanced mammal such as man is based on information formulated in a number of different media: notably the genetic and the cultural ones. This must also be true of the behaviour of societies which are composed of families and individuals. If this information constitutes, in each case, a single organisation or model — which has come into being as a result of the normal developmental process (proceeding from the general to the particular by means of steps occurring in a specific sequence and by the process of differentiation), then genetic and cultural information must develop according to the same rules and *can only be studied in terms of the same single scientific discipline*, as must also the *associated behaviour pattern.* This of course makes nonsense of the distinction between the natural sciences and the social sciences, and shows the inadequacy of present-day reductionist scientific method, in terms of which it is impossible to understand the behaviour of complex systems, in particular social ones.

### Levels of Organisation
The notion of levels of organisation used by biologists can be shown to be applicable to the development of societies. The principle is a simple one. Particular types of organisation can provide the basis of growth within

certain limits. A point is eventually reached, however, at which further growth ceases to be possible for reasons of communication and control, in particular because the specific set of bonds exploited to ensure the cohesion of the system cannot be extended to hold together any more sub-systems, for all bonds, whether they be those which hold together the nucleus of an atom, or a human society, have *limited extendability*. When the point is reached at which further growth becomes impossible, the systems must join together to form a larger system, whose cohesion will be ensured by a new set of bonds, and whose control will be maintained by a new and more elaborate control mechanism. Thus, atoms cannot expand beyond a certain point. Eventually they join together to form a molecule and a new level of organisation has been reached. The same is true when molecules join together to form a cell; and when cells join together to form a multicellular organism. With the develoment of sexual reproduction, a new level of organisation is achieved: that of the family. Often, the family is of a temporary nature. As the amount of information that has to be communicated from one generation to the next, via the cultural learning process, increases, however, so the family becomes permanent — as it is with man.

This process coincides with the development of what has been called 'retardation' — the slowing down of the developmental process so that it can become more highly differentiated in time. *This is the more pronounced the more advanced the species, reaching its culmination point in man, for whom the family is undoubtedly the basic unit of social organisation — so much so, that if it is not present, no other social structures can possibly develop.*

# 2 The Family Basis of Social Structure

**The Family, a Definition**

Until recently, it has been fashionable to maintain that other forms of human social organisation are more fundamental than the family. The original unit of human organisation was taken to be the primaeval horde, like that of the baboons. This is one of Freud's assumptions[19] (and also one of Trotter's[20]) and is implicit in his theory of man's social development, which began when the sexually deprived bachelors rose against their overbearing Pasha-like fathers. This myth was exploded* by Malinowski,[21] who writes:

"Very often it is assumed by anthropologists that humanity developed from a gregarious simian species and that man inherited from his animal ancestors the so-called 'herd-instincts'. Now this hypothesis is entirely incompatible with the view here taken that common sociability develops by extension of the family bonds and from no other sources."

Murdock[22] also regards this principle as fundamental:

"Unlike the ants and bees, man is not biologically a social animal equipped by heredity with prepotent capacities for complex associative life, but in every individual case must be bent and broken to group living through the arduous process of socialisation and be kept in the paths of conformity through the imposition of social controls. The first anthropologist fully to appreciate this basic fact was Malinowski with his emphasis upon the factor of 'reciprocity' in the maintenance of norms of interaction."

Tinbergen[23] comes to the same conclusion looking at the problem from a very different point of view. He writes:

---

* The Oedipus Complex, to which Freud attaches so much importance, only makes sense in a patrilineal society. About forty per cent of known societies are matrilineal. In such a society, there is no father figure who both exerts authority over the child and sleeps with the child's mother. The individual who behaves in a 'fatherly' manner towards the child and is head of the household is the senior male in the mother's lineage group (usually her brother, sometimes her father) and therefore has no sexual relations with her. Hence the Oedipus complex cannot arise. Malinowski had a long controversy with Ernest Jones on this subject.

"Contrary to current thought, there is not in my opinion a social instinct in the sense in which we normally understand it. There are no special activities which we can call social and which do not already form part of some other instinct. There is nothing to make us believe that there is at work a system of centres controlling social activities."

In other words, the information and corresponding instructions that will make man a family animal are transmitted from one generation to the next; while those that will make of him a social animal must be developed during the process of socialisation. That is what education is for — a fact our educationalists have long lost sight of. [24] *The information necessary for man to become a social animal is thus of a cultural nature, rather than of a genetic one.* However, since the total information pattern that will determine the behaviour of a social system constitutes a single whole, organised hierarchically from the general to the particular (the latter information having developed from the former by the process of differentiation), *it follows that the general instructions that have made of man a social animal must be derived from those that made of him a family animal.* What is more, by virtue of the rules of behavioural development, one must also assume that *these instructions will provide serious constraints on his range of possible adaptations.* It is for this reason that we find the same cultural strategies exploited over and over again in parts of the world that have had no contact with each other, just as is the case with biological strategies — hence, cultural convergence (see Appendix IV).

## The Universality of the Human Family

Before we follow this line of argument any further, we must establish *that the family is universal among stable societies;* otherwise, in terms of the basic principles of development stated above, no society would be possible. The universality of the family was established by Murdock[25] on the basis of a sample of 250 cultures, figuring in the Yale Cross-Cultural Index. This assumes his definition of the family as satisfying "sexual or reproductive, educational and economic requirements".

Are there any exceptions to this principle? A number have been proposed. The first is from Melford Spiro[26] who considers that the family has largely been dispensed with in the Israeli kibbutzim. This does not appear to be a serious objection. Firstly, the kibbutz is probably a transient form of social organisation. There is no evidence that it is stable. It is in any case a contrived one, in the sense that it has not developed by what might be called a 'cultural evolution', but has simply been established as an experimental social form. Also, it is by no means certain that the family has in fact entirely been dispensed with. The kibbutz has undoubtedly taken over a number of the roles normally fulfilled by the family, such as the educative one (which in our own society has been

15

taken over by the State), but the family still provides, to a certain extent at least, the protective environment within which the earlier phases of the socialisation process must occur. There is a more interesting exception, however, namely the Nayars of the Malabar coast, in what is now the Indian state of Kerala.[27]

The Nayars are a matrilineal and matrilocal people. They live in extended matrilineal families run by the oldest male (*karanavan*). These extended families are organised into lineages. In the old days, every two years, these lineages would hold a grand ceremony at which all the girls who had reached puberty would be ritually married with men drawn from specific lineages with which theirs were linked. At these ceremonies the girls were presented with certain ritual gifts including a gold necklace referred to as a *tali*. Following the ceremony, the girls were isolated with their husbands and deflowered, though this was apparently not a necessary part of the ceremony. Thenceforward the girl's status changed. She was called *Amma*, meaning mother, and allowed to have children — not by the ritual husband who need have no further contact with either her or her children , but by her lovers. These were referred to as *sambadham*. She could have as many as she liked though they had to be of the appropriate sub-caste and outside her lineage. When she became pregnant it was essential that one of them should acknowledge probable paternity, which was done by providing a fee of a cloth and some vegetables to the midwife. If no such acknowledgement was forthcoming, it was assumed that the girl had had relations with a man of lower caste or with a Christian or a Moslem. This meant her expulsion from her society. The duties of the *sambadham* from then onwards were limited to providing his mistress with gifts at festivities. He had nothing to do with the maintenance of the mother or the upbringing of the child, which was the duty of the *karanavan*, the chief male matrilineal relative. The children's duties to the *tali* husband were limited to mourning at his death. The *sambadham* — whether the progenitor or not — were addressed as *accahan* or Lord, but no kinship terms extended to their family and no mourning was observed at their death.

This organisation has defied customary classification. Many have maintained that it provides an exception to the principle of the universality of the family. Others (Murdock included) doubt whether this account of Nayar organisation is authentic.

The reason why it presents a classificatory problem is that our method of classification is wrong. We are accustomed to think of the family as consisting of a father, a mother, and some children, with possibly one or two grandparents attached. Instead we should think of it *in terms of the functions it fulfils. The family would then be present if the family functions were fulfilled by individuals biologically and culturally adapted*

16

*to do so.* The community as a whole or a specialised institution would not qualify, for a family is a differentiated system at a particular level of organisation. Its functions must be fulfilled by individuals — and specific ones at that. The point is, however, that they need not all be fulfilled by the members of what we regard to be the family.

For each *different* function, in fact, the family system (seen functionally) can consist of a *different* set of individuals. Thus the first family function is to engender the child. Associated with this is that of satisfying sexual needs. Among the Nayars, the family system whose normal functioning achieved these ends was composed of a girl and the *sambadham.* The role of parents is to bestow upon the children the parental care and affection they require and to undertake the task of instilling in them the basic cultural values and of teaching them the fundamentals of the tasks they will have to fulfil in later life. Among the Nayars, this function was fulfilled by the mother and her matrilineal lineage headed by the *karanavan.* Last but not least, a child requires an identity or a social status, the basis of which the family can alone provide — a point neglected by Murdock in his definition of the family. This was achieved by yet a third social system, that composed of the girl and her *tali* husband. Thus, the essential family functions were fulfilled in the case of the Nayar *by three different social groupings.* If we regard this as abnormal, it is only that in our Western society they tend to be fulfilled (in so far as they are fulfilled at all) *by a single social grouping which we call the family.*

What is more, it can be shown that the same principle holds for larger groups than the family. Thus, after reviewing the different criteria for determining what constitutes a political unit, Lucy Mair[5] writes, ''there are some societies of which it is difficult to say that there is one political community for all purposes.'' Thus a tribe, which is often endogamous and hence the unit of behaviour for marital purposes, is divided into different lineages which are often the effective units of political life, which may themselves be paired off into moieties. These may or may not correspond with the village, which will be the unit of behaviour for a large number of social and economic functions, etc. In addition, the men in particular will be divided into age groups, each with a particular function, which in turn may form part of wider age classes — the young, the adolescents and the elders. Furthermore, there will tend to be secret societies which are units of behaviour for magical and ritualistic purposes and working groups which will be the units of behaviour for various economic functions.

### How is the Family Held Together?

The functions fulfilled within the family are designed to satisfy the needs of all the parties concerned. Thus, a father *needs* to behave in a fatherly way as much as a child requires that his father should do so (see the Hierarchical Cooperation Principle). The members of the family are thereby dependent on each other. It is this dependence which provides the bonds that hold the family together.

There are a number of different family bonds, such as those that hold together a father with his daughter, a mother with her son, a mother with her daughter, a man with his younger brother, a girl with her younger sister, a brother with his sister. These bonds are all different and also *asymmetrical*. The relationship of a father to his daughter, for instance, is very different from that of a daughter to her father.[22] The relationship of a father to his children differs even more noticeably from the mother's relationship with her children. According to Fromm: "The love of a mother for her child, antecedent to that of the father, appears to be an unconditional love, whereas that of the father is conditional to the child's 'good' behaviour or achievements."[28]

This is reflected in the different relationships between a society and the gods it worships. As Fromm notes, it is no coincidence that most undisciplined and self-indulgent cultures have turned to a mother goddess, whereas more virile peoples, wishing to be judged according to their moral worth and their achievements, have chosen a paternal symbol as their chief deity (*See page 50*).

What is important is that the basic differences between these bonds are exploited to determine culturally differentiated behaviour. *It is only by maintaining this differentiation that cooperation is possible and that the society can display order or negative-entropy.*

### The Exploitation of the Family Bonds
The fact that we tend to classify our social and physical environment in terms of the classificatory system applied to the different members of the family should be evident from our personal experience.

Tinbergen[23] shows that we view our domestic pets in this way. Dogs with snub noses and high foreheads are particularly popular among women requiring a child surrogate. Similarly, behaviour towards political leaders can only be understood if the latter are interpreted as fathers, husbands, lovers, sons, grandsons, brothers, etc. One whose image does not permit such classification has little political future, indeed.

Even consumer products are regarded in this way. A camera with a huge telescopic lens dangling over the belly of a dashing young photographer is clearly regarded as an extension to his penis by admiring girls. In this connection, I remember a cartoon of a dapper little man with pince-nez hesitating at the motor-show between a staid family model and a fast sports car. The salesman was saying, "Well, Sir, it all depends whether you want a wife or a mistress.''

We have already noted that we regard the gods we worship as fathers, mothers, and children; what is not generally recognised, however, is that subconsciously we see the individual members of our community in much the same way.

## Kinship Terminology

The fact that the family bonds are extended to embrace the members of the community is reflected in the elaborate kinship terminology developed by tribal societies, and in terms of which the whole community is classified. In this way a classificatory system, as Radcliffe Brown[29] points out, "may be applied over a wide range of relationships. Thus a first cousin of the father, being his father's brother's son, whom he therefore calls 'brother', is classified with the father and the same term 'father' is applied to him. His son in turn, a second cousin, is called 'brother'. By this process of extension of the principle of classification, nearer and more distant collateral relatives are arranged into a few categories and a person has many relatives to whom he applies the term 'father' or 'mother' or 'brother' or 'sister'.''

The most important feature of these classificatory terminologies was pointed out long ago by Sir Henry Maine.[30] "The effect of the system,'' he wrote, "is in general to bring within your mental grasp a much greater number of your kindred than is possible under a system to which we are accustomed. In other words, the classificatory terminology is primarily a mechanism which facilitates the establishment of wide-range systems of kinship.''

What is more, "the attitude and behaviour of a person towards a particular person,'' as Radcliffe Brown[29] observes, "is affected not only by the category to which he belongs but also by the degree of nearness or distance of the relationship. In classificatory systems there are many women whom a particular man calls 'sister'. In some systems he will be prohibited from marrying these women. In some others he may not marry any 'near sister', i.e., any one of these women who is related to him within a certain degree of cognatic relationship, but may marry a more distant 'sister'.''

The important thing is that if people are referred to by different names *there is a reason for it*, and the reason appears to be that different names reflect expected differences in behaviour towards the people they refer to. Likewise, if two people are given the same name, it implies that the sort of behaviour due to both of them is the same. This is also the conclusion of Radcliffe Brown:[29] "I hold that all over the world there are important correspondences between kinship nomenclature and social practices.''

In other words the elaborate kinship terminology used by tribal peoples reflects the fact that a tribal society is a highly differentiated system in which each individual has a specific identity and a specific role in terms of which it is only possible to understand the complex set of relationships between him and all the other members of his society.

## The Community

If the family is universal, so is the community.[22] This is basically a group of families living together. It occurs in every known human society (even among the Eskimos, who, though they live in family groups throughout the summer, gather together with other family groups during the winter months).[31] Communities have gone under various names. Among nomadic hunter gatherers, who have made up probably more than 90 per cent of the people who have ever lived on this planet, they tend to be referred to as bands. They differ from the communities of sedentary peoples, in that they tend to be less permanent. Communities can be made up of anything from fifty to a thousand or so people. The upper limit is set, in the words of Linton,[32] by "the practical impossibility of establishing close contacts with and developing habitual attitudes towards any greater number of people."

How are the family bonds exploited to hold together the community, and to give rise to still larger units?

## The Clan

One device for exploiting the family bonds is to divide the society into clans which transcend other groupings. According to Murdock,[22] the clan appears to be present in at least half of the traditional societies examined. "Whereas the community is made up of consanguinal and affinal relatives, the clan will be made up of consanguinal ones, either traced on the mother's side (matriclan), on the father's side (patriclan), or very occasionally via the uncle (avuncuclan)." Both groupings will be made up of people of different sexes and of different age groups held together by a complete set of family bonds. It is not surprising that they will simply be replicas of the family unit on a larger scale.

In patrilineal and patrilocal societies, there will be a tendency towards an 'atomistic' organisation of society, with the creation of more clearly defined social units; thus each tribesman or citizen will belong to his father's kinship group and will also reside among his father's kinsmen.

Lowie[4] quotes the case of the Australian Deri, among whom descent is matrilineal but whose marriage is patrilocal. In this case the territorial unit exists with and is independent of the kinship unit. It is clear that as a result of this institution the different clans are closely linked to each other. Indeed, as a result of this, the Deri constitute a nation and have a paramount chief. This is not the case, however, of the Kanera, who are in other respects a similar people, but are patrilineal and patrilocal. The divisions between the clans in their case are much greater, there is no paramount chief, and in fact the Kanera do not constitute a political unit of any kind.

This provides an interesting illustration of the variety of different social systems which can be built up by exploiting the basic family bonds in the appropriate way.

What is important is that, whenever a full set of family bonds is exploited to create a social unit other than a family, the larger unit will invariably reflect the family's structure, since *the family provides the only model for holding it together.*

## Larger Society Reflects Basic Communal Structure

In traditional tribal and supra-tribal groupings, when the social unit is larger than the local community, secondary groupings clearly reflect the basic ones of family, clan and tribe. In Athens, the army was originally organised in exactly the same way. In the *Iliad*, we find Nestor reminding Agamemnon of the rule to dispose of his men by tribes and phatries: "That phatry may assist phatry, and tribe may assist tribe." [33]

According to Glotz,[34] "all the public services, whether one considers the army, the navy, and what one may call the exchequer, respected the natural groupings, without which the city could not exist."

Basic social structure was also reflected in the structure and form of tribal and supra-tribal groupings, as pointed out by Linton.[32] Thus the Iroquois had a single basic pattern of formal control which extended from the household through clan, village and tribe to the League itself. They themselves recognised this continuity, referring to the League as the Long House and emphasising its similarity to a household. Again, the confederations of the Tuareg, with their noble and servile tribes, were a direct projection of the tribal organisation with its noble and serf families.

Linton writes:[32] "The transformations of such alliances into organised political units seems to require special conditions. The patterns of confederate governments are, almost without exception, projections of those of the tribal governments with which their members are familiar. While these patterns always have to be somewhat modified to meet the new conditions, there is a clearly recognisable continuity."

## Settlement Patterns

A traditional society's social structure is also reflected in its very well defined laws of residence. These will largely determine the nature of the bonds linking one person to another and, thereby, the character of the community. Whatever be these rules, the members of the community will be related to each other, or at least, and this is more important, they will *regard* themselves as related to each other.

The arrangement of the houses in a traditional village also reflects its social structure.[35] That is why transforming a local village so that it conforms to the Western model and forcing the inhabitants to live in modern housing estates or townships causes such terrible social disruption. This is pointed out by Levi-Strauss[36] with reference to the Bororo of Brazil and also by Robert Jaulin[37] with reference to the Motilone Indians on the frontier between British Guiana and Brazil.

## Land Tenure

The same principle applies to land tenure. A man has a right to a specific piece of land because of his specific position within the social group. In ideal conditions the pattern of land tenure reflects the society's social structure.[38]

In all cases, as Sir Henry Maine pointed out,[30] *the land is an aspect of the group, but not the basis of grouping*. A man does not derive his status from the ownership of a piece of land, but rather obtains ownership of a piece of land by virtue of his status. Land tenure, in fact, is based on *status* not on *contract*. Since this status reflects a man's exact position in his society's social structure, the latter must be faithfully reflected in its principles of land tenure.

## Economic and Social Units Coincide

Not surprisingly, in a traditional society, the units of economic activity tend to coincide with those into which man is organised for all other social requirements, i.e., the family and the community. With us, a man's social position is to a certain extent, and possibly increasingly determined by his economic position. In a traditional society it is the other way around. "He tends to hold his economic position in virtue of his social position. Hence to displace him economically means a social disturbance."[39]

We have described how, in general, the basic social structure underlying the organisation of the traditional community is reflected in all its activities. This was undoubtedly the case in Rome until late in its history. In the classical world, however, changes occurred which made survival of traditional social forms increasingly difficult. Societies became bigger, empires were established, mobility increased, and certain activities, such as warfare, trade, and industry, began to play so important a role that the natural balance within a traditional society became seriously impaired. As this occurred, normal rules of residence determining the social structure of communities and their relationship with other key groupings, such as the clan, were subordinated to new, usually economic, considerations. Social order gave way to social randomness or entropy. The basic units of society ceased to be highly differentiated and self-regulating natural systems and increasingly became random groups of individuals held together by what bond is afforded by sheer contiguity and via the agency of governmental institutions, i.e. asystemic controls. In Athens, this situation led to the famous reforms of Cleithenes in 409 B.C. by which the *deme* became the basic administrative unit of the Athenian State.

In the same way the Roman *gens,* originally a kinship group, eventually became a territorial unit, in spite of which the fiction of common ancestry was for a long time maintained.

Among the ancient Jews the same reforms were made by King Solomon.[40] The country was divided into territorial units which did not in fact coincide with the ancient tribal territories. It seems that some of the tribes actually came into existence in this way, since they appear to have been named after the district which they occupied, (Gillead, Benjamin, Ephraim). Lods[40] writes, "The early groupings, based originally on consanguinity (natural or artificial), tended to become territorial aggregations. The clan finally became synonymous with the population of a town . . . Membership of a tribe consisted not in descent to a particular individual but in belonging by birth to a particular territory." Once settled in Canaan, the Israelites soon reached the stage of the peasants of Khorassan, of whom the Arabs say contemptuously: 'their villages are their pedigrees'. Calif Omar urged his Arabs to preserve their pedigree and not to become like the peasants of Iraq, who, to the question, 'Whence art thou?' (i.e. from what tribe?), were wont to reply, 'from such-and-such a village'.

Thus, Lods tells us that among the Jews, even after the establishment of the tribes as geographical units, "the tribes also retained their faith in genealogies, however fictitious these might be, and in their rival claims to pre-eminence, as exemplified for instance in the arrangement of the sons of Jacob in the official genealogy and in the jibes directed against various tribes in certain early poems."[40]

As Lods points out, rather than accept the facts of new social groupings, they "imposed their own social framework upon the population of the country."[40]

Among the Mexicans, according to Thompson, "at the time of the Aztec collapse, the clans or *calpulli* functioned more as geographic units than as units based on kinship."[41]

It is probable that, as these territorial associations ceased to reflect the basic family structure, they also ceased to constitute viable social units, for it meant that the complex set of bonds capable of holding them together had become seriously eroded.

## Secondary Groupings
The extension of the family bonds to link together all the members of a

23

stable community requires the exploitation of still more subtle cultural devices. Most notably, the community is bound together by a veritable cobweb of secondary associations of different sorts.

Durkheim[42] fully realised that a society could only be held together if organised hierarchically into groups and sub-groups; that a society, in fact, could only be built up by associating smaller units among which effective bonds could be created, and that these bonds were necessary not only to create the societies, but to satisfy the special requirements of their individual members (the Hierarchical Cooperation Principle). Thus, he writes: "A nation can be maintained only if, between the State and the individual, there is intercalated a whole series of secondary groups near enough to the individuals to attract them strongly in their sphere of action and drag them, in this way, into the general torrent of social life."

The absence of these 'secondary groupings', according to Durkheim, is one of the principle reasons for the instability of the modern Nation State.

Durkheim was particularly impressed with the structure of Roman and later Medieval trade associations. Indeed, Roman trade guilds were formed on the same model as the family and the *gens*, with a religious centre and a patron deity. They were referred to as *collegia* dedicated to Minerva, the goddess of handiwork. Their development is traced very carefully by Durkheim.[42]

According to Waltzing,[43] the guilds were primarily religious organisations. "Each one had its particular god whose cult was celebrated in a special temple when the means were available. In the same way as each family had its *lar* and *familiaris*, each city its *genius publicus*, each organisation had its protective god, *genius collegii*.

"Naturally, this occupational cult did not dispense with celebrations, with sacrifices and banquets in common . . . As corollary to this religious character, the organisation of workmen was, at the same time, a burial society. United in a cult during their lives, like the Gentiles, the members of these populations also wished to rest together after death."

Durkheim[42] then asks: "A common cult, common banquets, a common cemetery, all united together — are these not all the distinctive characteristics of the domestic organisation at the time of the Romans? Thus it has been said that the Roman population was a great family. The community of interests took the place of a community of blood." This view is shared by Waltzing[43] who notes that "The members looked upon themselves as brothers even to the extent of calling themselves by that name . . . The protectors of the organisation often took the names of father and mother."

Other secondary groupings that we may consider include age grades and military organisations.

## Age Grades

The division of a society into age grades is common to most traditional societies. This division plays an essential role in education, since in proceeding from one age grade to the next the child is subjected to that ordered sequence of different influences that will ensure its socialisation or education (see the Sequential Principle). At the same time, and by the same token, the different age grades provide the basis for the most fundamental specialisation of functions within a traditional society. Also, membership of a common age grade creates one of the most powerful social bonds. As Lowie[4] writes: "Simultaneous initiation creates ties transcending the bonds due to equal status."

Among the Masai warriors and pastoralists of East Africa, according to Lowie, the boys and immature girls are separated from the rest of the community. During the period of the initiation to enable a boy to rank as a warrior, he is a neophyte. For the first two years following this, he is an apprentice (shaved one); then he figures as a fully-fledged Brave, until he is about 29, when he marries, leaves the bachelor's *kraal*, and assumes for the remainder of his life the dignity of an Elder. Special clothes and emblems distinguish certain periods. Each age class must assert itself by its prowess in war, and to this end there is a great deal of competition with the other age classes.

The bonds exploited to hold together age grades can only be those which hold together brothers of the same family. Indeed, as could be expected, their members refer to each other as brothers.

## Military Organisations

Among warlike societies a strong social bond is that existing between different members of the same military clubs. Among the Crow Indians, it is said that there were originally eight of these. The number dwindled to four: the muddy hands; the big dog; the foxes; and the lumpwoods. From the 70s onwards, only the last two were in full vigour. Each society had its dance and song and distinctive badges. Membership was independent of clan and entry was informal. The organisation was extremely complicated and involved much ritual. The 'foxes' club is described in detail by Lowie.[4] It is clear from his description how important was the role played in the life of the Crow by these clubs. Their ambitions and motivations were influenced by them to an enormous extent, whereas ordinary egoistic preoccupations or family ones were submerged by the desire for success or prestige in these associations.

## Criss-Cross Linkages

In this way every member of the tribe is closely associated in some way with every other member, for if a person is not associated with

25

another by being a member of the same family or clan, he is certain to be associated with him by belonging to the same military group, economic unit, secret society, etc. The members of a traditional society are thereby linked in a veritable cobweb of relationships in which all must be caught up in some way. A man has a status in each of the groupings to which he belongs and in any society his total status is, as Linton[32] writes, "the sum total of all the statuses which he occupies. It represents his position with relation to the total society." As a result of this particular structure of society, a man has a very definite status, which he lacks in a mass society such as ours.

This lack of status from which man suffers in mass society is what Durkheim calls 'anomie'. Marx and others have referred to the same phenomenon as 'alienation' — or loneliness in a crowd, which is so much worse than loneliness in a desert.

Each individual in a tribal society is a highly differentiated member of the society and, as a result, it functions as a highly differentiated system. Modern mass societies, by contrast, are merely assemblies of undifferentiated individuals held together by common institutions.


**The Role of Religion**

In our irreligious age, the importance of religion as a means of maintaining a society's social structure, and thereby assuring stable government, is grossly underrated.

We forget that, in a traditional society, religion is very much part of a society's culture, so much so as to be indissociable from it. Indicative of this is the fact that there is no word for 'religion' in the language of traditional societies. The reason is that there is simply no need for it. 'Religio' meant simply 'matters of state' — and it never occurred to anyone that these could be dealt with on any basis but that which we would refer to as religious. Why is religion so important? One of the answers is that the elaborate social structure of a traditional society, if it is to be maintained, must be sanctified, i.e. provided with a divine or supernatural protection. Empirically, this can be verified, since there is no instance of anything approaching a stable society among people who were not deeply religious, and whose religion was not an integral part of their culture, serving to regulate their behaviour towards their social and physical environment. In order to sanctify a society's social structure, the gods must be organised in such a way that they faithfully reflect it.

On this subject, Francis L.K. Hsu[44] shows that among the Chinese ". . . the world of the spirits is approximately a copy of, and strictly a supplement to, the world of the living." The same is true of all traditional societies. The family, the tribe, and other groupings are thereby religious units as well as social ones.

The important role of the father in most traditional societies is largely due to his position as head of the family cult, just as the importance of the tribal chief lay in his position as high priest of the tribe, and that of the king as high priest of the association of tribes, as in the ancient City State.

The religion of a traditional society also plays an important part in ensuring the continuity of the society. The gods are identified with the society's ancestors, and they are organised according to the same plan as the living, for they are considered to have retained their social identity even in death. A tribal society is said to be made up of the living, the dead, and the yet to be born — i.e. it has total continuity.

## Religion in a Disintegrating Society

Since the organisation of the gods reflects a society's structure, it is not surprising that the disintegration of a society is accompanied by a change in the structure of its pantheon. The principal god finds himself isolated. Instead of being but *primus inter pares*, he is now alone and reigns supreme. Also, with the disintegration of its culture, the society loses precisely those features that distinguish it from its neighbours, and, as a result, the realm of the principal god slowly spreads. From being a tribal god, he gradually develops into a universal one.

As this occurs, so religion loses its social functions. Slowly it becomes simply an institution for providing solace to increasingly alienated individuals.

Robertson Smith[45] traces the beginning of the idea of a universal god among the Semites to a phenomenon he refers to as 'Clienthood to God' which slowly arose with the breakdown of social structures and the increased promiscuity of people that followed the development of trade. He writes, "Hereditary priesthoods of Arabian sanctuaries were often in the hands of families that did not belong to the tribe of worshippers but were apparently descended from older inhabitants, and in such cases the modern worshippers were only clients of a foreign god."

The same tendency is seen in the development of the practice of pilgrimage to foreign shrines. "Almost all Arabia met at Mecca, and the shrine of Hierapolis drew visitors from the whole Semitic world."[45] Unlike the family gods of tribal society, these foreign gods were too remote to have a permanent and pervading influence upon the daily life of society. The gods had become distinct from the social structure; they could no longer serve to sanctify the family as a unit, nor the moral behaviour of the Islamic people.

In this respect, the Islamic state offers a perfect contrast to the ancient Hellenic city. The Hellenic city was made up of families. The original pre-Solonic and pre-Lycurgan legal codes reflected the importance of the family; crimes committed by an individual were considered the responsibility of his family and compensation had to be paid to the family of the victims. In this respect, Hellenic law was similar to that of primitive man. In neither case did the individual have any specific existence except as a member of a family and of a clan.

The clans were organised as the tribes which in turn were organised into the city state. Theseus, who was considered the founder of Athens, was in fact the king responsible for unifying the tribes. The notion of duty was all-dominating. Duty was due to the family, to the clan, to the tribe, and to the city. The duty to the gods was important because the gods too were members of the same social units.

Von Grunebaum[46] points to the essential characteristic of Islamic society, i.e., the substitution of religious affiliation for kinship as a rationale of social organisation. Apart from economic considerations, the inhabitants had in common the fact that they shared a common religion. The result of this was that they had no duty towards their fellow men and hence their community. Whereas the Hellenic state was characterised by a high level of honesty and integrity, there was nothing in the Islamic state to prevent each man from exploiting his neighbour.

So stable was the Hellenic state in its hey-day that the mechanisms of government were reduced to the minimum, and there was nothing to correspond to the modern police force, which is required to maintain precarious order in heterotelic communities. The Hellenes prided themselves on the fact that their cities were run by the citizens. In the Islamic state the citizens had no hand in government. In the Hellenic state public opinion was the sovereign power. *Demoukratos* was not an empty phrase nor a legalistic fiction, but the institutionalisation of *Demouphemos*, i.e. public opinion. In the Islamic state, public opinion was of no account; the public was broken up into a mass of individuals and did not form a homeotelic unit capable of expressing itself.

In the Hellenic state there was, as a result, a tradition of self-government. Tyrants were infrequent and their advent to power was considered the worst fate that could overcome a city. In the Islamic state, on the other hand, tyranny has always been the only known form of government. In the Hellenic state the centre of the city was the Agora; a city without an Agora was inconceivable to the Greeks. In the Islamic state the Agora was replaced by the Mosque. This clearly symbolises how duty to the community was replaced by duty to God.*

* In fact, the Moslem town was not a body politic at all, any more than is a modern Nation State. "A given town," as Von Grunebaum writes, "may at a given moment enjoy independence or self-government, in the sense that it is not subjected to an outside power of whose territory it forms but one part. Sovereignty and freedom may fall to it accidentally, as it were; self-government with executive officials designated by the full citizens there never could be, for the city constituted not a closed corporation, a share in which defines the citizen, but merely a function-

## The Social Structure of the Physical Environment

If a society is to function as a natural self-regulating system, it must be able to respond to its environment with a behaviour pattern that constitutes a single integrated whole. Such a behaviour pattern will only be possible if the society has at its disposal a single integrated model of its relationship with the environment, a model which is to be achieved by classifying the *total* environment in terms of the same basic classificatory system.

If we look at our modern States, we see that the different aspects of their behaviour are almost entirely unconnected with each other. Although there are other factors involved, the situation is made inevitable by the division of science into separate watertight compartments, between which there is only the most superficial contact. Tribal man does not turn to a compartmentalised science for an understanding of his physical environment; instead, he classifies its constituent parts in terms of the classificatory system which he uses for the members of his society and the gods that make up his pantheon. Because of the fundamental importance which he attaches to the structure of his society, he cannot conceive of any part of his environment as not organised in a similar fashion.

Durkheim and Mauss[47] surveyed the systems used by the Australian aborigines, the Zuni and Sioux Indians, and the Chinese to classify the natural world. Noting the common belief that man began to conceive things by relating them to himself, they argue that the schemes they have considered are characterised not so much by anthropocentricity as by sociocentricity. "The centre of the first schemes of nature is not the individual: it is society. Nothing shows this more clearly than the way in which the Sioux retain the whole universe, in a way, within the limits of tribal space, and we have seen how universal space itself is nothing more than the site occupied by the tribe, only indefinitely extended beyond its real limits. It is by virtue of the same mental disposition that so many peoples have placed the centre of the world, 'the navel of the earth', in their own political or religious capital, i.e. at the place which is the centre of their moral life. Similarly, but in another order of ideas, the creative force of the universe and everything in it was first conceived as a mythical ancestor, the generator of the society."

The Zuni system of classifying the natural environment is an excellent illustration of sociocentricity. According to Durkheim and Mauss, "what we find among the Zuni is a veritable arrangement of the universe. All

ally unified, administrative entity with a more or less stable complement of settlers or inhabitants. To such cities Plato's characterization of certain states as 'merely aggregations of men dwelling in cities who are the subjects and servants of a part of their own state' could fittingly be applied. There were no qualifications to be met to obtain admission to citizenship in the Moslem town for the simple reason that there was no body of town dwellers in whom political or civic authority was seen to reside."[46]

beings and facts in nature, 'the sun, moon and stars, the sky, earth and sea, in all their phenomena and elements; and all inanimate objects, as well as plants, animals and men, are classified, labelled and assigned to fixed places in a unique and integrated system', in which all the parts are coordinated and subordinated one to another by 'degrees of resemblance'.

"In the form in which we now find it, the principle of this system is a division of space into seven regions: north, south, west, east, zenith, nadir, and the centre. Everything in the universe is assigned to one or other of these seven regions."[47]

These regions appear to coincide with the main divisions of Zuni society. In the words of Durkheim and Mauss, "this division of the world is exactly the same as that of the clans within the pueblo."

In industrial societies, sociocentricity has given way to egocentricity: the physical environment is no longer classified in terms of social structures that have largely disintegrated, but rather in terms of the experience of their alienated individual members, and the society is no longer under control.

**Conclusion and Implications**
To understand the true function and importance of the family, it is necessary to view it cross-culturally (see Appendix VI) and cross-behaviourally, and in terms of the basic theoretical principles underlying the behaviour of natural systems at all levels of organisation — i.e. in terms of a General Model of Behaviour, embryonic though it may be at the present time. In doing this it becomes clear that the family is the basic unit of social behaviour. This means that its development constitutes the earliest, most general, and most important phase of the process leading to the development of a society and its renewal with each generation — a process we have referred to as 'sociosynthesis'. This stage will colour all subsequent ones (the Generality Principle). If it does not occur, then the process as a whole will not occur — or more precisely, it will not constitute an integral whole, which is required if it is to be adaptive, i.e. if it is to tend towards stability (the Sequential Principle).

Seen slightly differently, as 'sociosynthesis' proceeds, so new levels of organisation are achieved. As in phylogeny, a higher level cannot be achieved without first passing through the intermediary ones. Thus, if there is no cell there can be no biological organism. *In the same way, if there is no family, there can be no community.*

By examining the process whereby families are associated to form a community, we see why this must be so. Firstly, it is only by exploiting that set of asymmetrical bonds which link together the different members of the family that the members of a community can be associated with each other to form an effective community. Secondly, it is only in terms of that classificatory system applied to the different members of the family that members of the community can be classified, and that, as a result, the community can be viewed as a differentiated system displaying a high degree of order or negative-entropy.

It is also in terms of the same classificatory system that a society's gods, and also, to a certain extent, its physical environment are classified. *Only in this way can a society's world-view provide it with a single integrated model of its relationship with its total environment.*

With the breakdown of the extended family, the classificatory system based upon it, inevitably, breaks down. As this occurs, the society comes increasingly to be regarded as consisting of largely independent individuals. There is a progressive erosion of those constraints which must be imposed on the individual's behaviour if it is to be compatible with the survival of the family and the community.

As attitudes change, the physical environment is no longer seen sociocentrically, but comes to be regarded egocentrically in terms of its capacity to satisfy individual (heterotelic) needs. At the same time, the gods are called upon increasingly to provide catharsis for socially deprived individuals and lose their socially and ecologically stabilising functions.

The result is that the society is deprived of continuity, both with regard to its own past experience and in its relationship with the environment. In fact the society finally ceases to constitute a system at all — it is simply a mass of socially unrelated individuals among whom a semblance of order, however superficial, can only be maintained by means of increasingly powerful external or asystemic controls: bureaucracies, dictators, etc. *These are no substitute for the internal or systemic controls which alone can maintain social stability.*

In the absence of systemic controls, those who dominate the society increase its instability by adopting expedients that favour their own short-term interests at the expense of the long-term interests of the society as a whole. These expedients are likely to be increasingly destructive as the problems that arise become more serious, and as the technology available for their implementation becomes more sophisticated. Furthermore, as the world is drawn into the orbit of the industrial system, social and ecological instabilities increase on a global scale — and are likely to continue until they lead to socio-economic collapse.

# 3 The Religion of a Stable Society

We all think that we know what is meant by religion, yet if we were asked to define it, we would probably all do so differently. In the irreligious age in which we live, many would agree with Salomon Reinach that it is but "a body of scruples which impede the fullest exercise of our faculties",[48] or even with Marx, who, as is well known, described it as "the opium of the people".

To both these critics, religion is some sort of aberration, one which may characterise backward, barbarous and ignorant people, but which, it is intimated, has no place in an advanced, civilised and enlightened society. In this paper I shall show that the opposite is in fact the case.

First of all, however, let us consider a few more definitions of religion. Thouless considers it as "a felt, practical relationship with what is believed in as a superhuman being or beings",[49] while Frazer regards it as "a propitiation or conciliation of powers superior to man which are believed to direct and control the course of nature and human life."[50]

They thus see religion as something which is intimately concerned with the supernatural.

Huxley describes it as "a reaction of a personality as a whole to its universe as a whole."[51] This is clearly a much wider definition, which includes, among other things, the notion of culture.

I regard the last three definitions as containing some of the essential elements of religion, although they do not provide a functional definition that is of use in developing a cross-cultural model of human social behaviour.[52]

I shall try to provide such a definition. *Religion I shall take as the control-mechanism of a stable society.*

## What is Control?

Let us begin by examining the nature of control. If we control a motor car or a guided missile, we keep it on its right course. Similarly, to control the behaviour pattern of a natural system (by which I mean a unit of behaviour within the biosphere such as a cell, a biological organism, an ecosystem, a society, etc.) means simply to keep it on its right course. This assumes that *it has a right course*, i.e., that it is goal-directed. The only alternative is to assume that it is purely random, which is clearly not the case (if it were purely random, we would be unable to study it).[10]

What is this goal? The answer is: the maintenance of stability. A system is regarded as stable if it is capable of maintaining its basic structure in the face of change. This means, among other things, taking those measures necessary to reduce the extent of possible changes. A system can only function in an environment approximately the same as that to which it has been adapted by its evolution and if changes get out of hand, the system is no longer able to function; it is no longer, in fact, under control.

This notion clearly conflicts with the dogma of man's infinite adaptability. By means of this dogma, industrial society seeks to justify its systematic efforts to modify its environment so that it diverges ever further from that in which it has evolved.[15] The dogma is based upon a failure to distinguish between stability, which implies long-term equilibrium, and a position (or a series of positions) of short-term equilibrium achieved at the cost of creating circumstances favouring more serious and more frequent discontinuities in the future. The supposedly adaptive behaviour of industrial man can only achieve short-term equilibrium.

We have said that stable systems tend towards the avoidance of change. Anthropological studies have confirmed that stable societies are organised (by their cultural evolution) with this end in view. However, the mechanism by which societies achieve this end remains largely unexamined.

For the elucidation of this mechanism, we must turn to the relatively new discipline of cybernetics, the study of control. Cybernetics has probably contributed more to the understanding of the behaviour of systems than any other discipline, by demonstrating that there is only one way to control the behaviour of a system, regardless of its level of organisation. The essential requirement is the presence of a control mechanism which operates by detecting data essential to the maintenance of the system's stable relationship with its environment, transducing them into the appropriate medium, and interpreting them in terms of the model which the system has built up of its relationship with its specific environment.[53]

Let us see how this principle operates at different levels of organisation. Consider the process of protein-synthesis. It is highly controlled, since it is a complicated and orderly process in which little is left to chance. What are the conditions required for its occurrence? Horowitz writes: "It seems evident that the synthesis of an enzyme — a giant protein molecule consisting of hundreds of amino-acid units arranged end

33

to end in a specific and unique order — requires a model or set of instructions of some kind. These instructions must be characteristic of the species; they must be automatically transmitted from generation to generation; and they must be constant yet capable of evolutionary change. The only known entity that could perform such a function is the gene. There are many reasons for believing that it transmits information by acting as a model or template."[12]

The mechanism ensuring the normal day-to-day behaviour of a biological organism, such as a dog or a man, must function in very much the same way. Kenneth Craik was probably the first person to point this out. He considered that the brain contained a model of the real world, in terms of which behaviour was mediated.[13]

We have seen that such a mechanism is required also to explain the behaviour of a human society. The model or template in this case is the society's world-view. It is in terms of this world-view that the society's behaviour pattern can be understood, and the two together are referred to as its culture. This view of culture implicitly underlies the approach to the study of traditional societies adopted by cultural ecology — a relatively new approach associated mainly with the names of Andrew Vayda and Roy Rappoport.

It may be objected that there are other means of controlling human societies. We, for instance, tend to suppose that a society is controlled by its institutional government on the basis of scientific and technological information. However, these are both relatively new principles, which have played but a negligible part in the total human experience of social control. What is more, they have failed, which was inevitable, since they do not satisfy any of the basic cybernetic requirements. By their very nature, they must lead society on a course — that upon which we are embarked today — which is diametrically opposed to the one which would ensure social stability and hence survival.

Indeed, the human experience during the historical period in which institutionalised government and objective knowledge were first utilised for social control has been one of wars, massacres, intrigues, famines — in other words, of precisely those discontinuities which social and ecological control should eliminate.

This era is in stark contrast to that which preceded it: during the Paleolithic, man's life appears to have been as stable and satisfying as that which is enjoyed by other forms of life on this planet until they are disturbed by man's disruptive activities.

### Requirements for the Control of a Human Society

What requirements must a religio-culture satisfy if it is to control the behaviour of a society? Firstly, it must be able to ensure that a society's

34

basic structure is maintained. The environment must be prevented from undergoing changes so great that the society cannot adapt to them without compromising its basic structure; and there must be continuity in the attitude of the society to its environment.

As is clear from the briefest of inspections, our religion today does not in any way satisfy these requirements. Religion plays little part in shaping our personal behaviour or that of our society. We tend simply to pay lip-service to the code of ethics which it teaches, while observing instead the very different code implicit in the culture of industrial society.

Although religious matters have now largely broken away from social ones, this has been true only for a very short time. To understand the phenomenon of religion, we must examine it in the light of the total human experience and not simply that of a small unrepresentative portion.

What few people today realise is that the religion of traditional societies, that is, the religion of man in his normal surroundings, admirably satisfies cybernetic requirements. *If we take religion as the basic social control mechanism, then the behaviour of traditional society can be described in terms of the basic cybernetic model which ensures the control of all other natural systems.*

## The Relationship between Religion and Society

One indication of the close relationship between religion and society is that, when a social group has come to adopt a particular religion, the motive has usually been social rather than religious. The object has been to re-establish the identity of the group in the face of foreign influences or those of a different and dominant socio-economic group, and to distinguish it from these and other groups.

Thus, in the kingdom of Ruanda, Catholicism was adopted for the purpose of providing a doctrine to hold together the Hutu revolutionaries against abusive Tutsi rule. In Burma, the Karen and Shan minorities were converted to Protestantism to affirm their national existence against the Burman Buddhist majority.

Messianic or Millenarist movements, of which there are about 7,000 in Africa alone today (in Lagos there is actually said to be a Trade Union of Messiahs), are created by an oppressed, socially and culturally deprived proletariat in an effort to establish a new system of values and an orderly society that will provide them with the social satisfactions they require and with an identity distinct from that of the mainstream society in which they have no place.

In many small American towns, the members of the different denominations are distinguished from each other not so much by the different set of theological beliefs that they might entertain, but rather by their social class. Thus the Episcopalians often make up the upper class, the Method-

35

ists the middle class, and the Baptists the lower class, while Pentecostalists, Holy Rollers and others are likely to belong to a sub-culture that is psychologically at least, antagonistic to the society as a whole. In this way each class will seek to constitute, albeit imperfectly, a separate cultural group, while living with the others in some sort of symbiotic relationship.

In traditional societies the social aspect of religion is very much more pronounced. Religion permeates all social life to the extent that it merges almost completely with the society's cultural pattern.

Fustel de Coulanges wrote of the ancient city: "This State and its religion were so totally fused that it was impossible not only to imagine the conflict between them, but even to distinguish one from the other."[:6]

The same can be said of traditional societies in Africa and Asia even today. In such a society it is possible to serve both gods and men, because there is no real distinction between the two. As between the natural and the supernatural or the sacred and the profane, the difference is one of degree rather than of kind.

I shall quote in full Robertson Smith's description[45] of the relationship between religion and traditional society:

"The circle into which a man was born was not simply a group of kinsfolk and fellow-citizens, but embraced also certain divine beings, the gods of the state, which to the ancient mind were as much a part of the particular community with which they stood connected as the human members of the social circle. The relationship between the gods of antiquity and their worshippers was expressed in the language of human relationship, and this language was not taken in a figurative sense but with strict literality. If a god was spoken of as father and his worshippers as his offspring, the meaning was that the worshippers were literally of his stock, that he and they made up one natural family with reciprocal family duties to one another. Or, again, if the god was addressed as king, and the worshippers called themselves his servants, they meant that the supreme guidance of the state was actually in his hands, and accordingly the organisation of the state included provision for consulting his will and obtaining his direction for all weighty matters, and also provision for approaching him as king with due homage and tribute.

"Thus a man was born into a fixed relation to certain gods as surely as he was born into relation to his fellow-men; and his religion, that is, the part of conduct which was determined by his relation to the gods, was simply one side of the general scheme of conduct prescribed for him by his position as a member of society. There was no separation between the spheres of religion and of ordinary life. Every social act had a reference to the gods as well as to men, for the social body was not made up of men only, but of gods and men."

What is more, Robertson Smith goes on to say:

"This account of the position of religion in the social system holds good, I believe, for all parts and races of the ancient world in the earlier stages of their history. The causes of so remarkable a uniformity lie hidden in the mists of prehistoric time, but must plainly have been of a general kind, operating on all parts of mankind without distinction of race and local environment; for in every region of the world, as soon as we find a nation or tribe emerging from prehistoric darkness into the light of authentic history, we find also that its religion conforms to the general type which has just been indicated."[45]

It is not surprising that, in such conditions, there was no word for religion. The Latin *religio*, for instance, meant 'matters of state', while in Japan the closest approximation, *Matsori Goro*, also meant government.

Let us examine more closely the model or world view in terms of which traditional man sees himself as related to the men and gods who form his social environment.

## Religio-Culture as a Means of Classifying the Members of the Social Environment

We live in a mass society in which the bonds that hold together traditional societies have been largely eroded. A mass society is an unstructured, undifferentiated aggregation of people. A traditional society, on the other hand, is a highly differentiated system: its members stand in clearly defined, asymmetrical relationships with one another and have distinct duties towards one another. Differentiation implies acknowledged social roles, and hence cooperation; in the absence of differentiation, a society will be characterised by competition and aggression.

Each member of a traditional society has at his disposal an elaborate kinship terminology, by means of which he classifies the members of his social environment; in some societies, there are as many as 150 different terms.

What is more, as Radcliffe Brown points out, there is a close correspondence between the designation of a relative by a specific term and the type of behaviour that must be displayed towards him.[29]

A religio-culture also allows the members of social groups other than one's own to be classified.

To understand this, we can take as an example the caste system in India, as described by Furnivall.[54] The religio-culture of a man's caste provides him with a complete model of the environment and a corresponding strictly prescribed behaviour pattern, determining every detail of his relationship with other members of his caste and with those outside it. The caste system supplies a religious basis for inequality: a man has no desire to advance himself other than by strict adherence to the behaviour appropriate to his caste. As a result, Furnivall argues, India "has main-

37

tained a stable plural society, in the face of overwhelming odds.''[54]

This example gives a clue to one of the basic functions of a religio-culture. *Religion ensures the stability of a traditional society by consecrating or sanctifying the generalities of its behaviour pattern.* As we have explained in detail elsewhere,* the generalities of a society's behaviour pattern embody those responses to its environment which have proved to be adaptive in the long term. If these generalities were to be disrupted, the consequences would be far-reaching and potentially catastrophic.

## The Classification of the Gods

Traditional man makes no distinction between his society and its pantheon. *Both are organised in exactly the same way.* What is more, the classificatory system is *four-dimensional*, so that both are regarded as forming part of a continuous series extending through time. *As a result, a society is capable of sanctifying its past and, hence, the social structure that it has inherited.* This ensures that the principles that have previously governed the society are strictly adhered to, a superb strategy for ensuring social continuity.

In traditional societies, the cultural information that is transmitted from one generation to the next represents not merely the experience of a single generation, but the total experience of a society stretching back into the mists of time. *In consequence, the principles governing the transmission of cultural information are precisely those governing the transmission of genetic information, which ensures the stability of natural systems at a biological level of organisation.*

As we have mentioned elsewhere, a traditional society, although it is often called a 'gerontocracy', or government by the old, is more properly described as a 'necrocracy', or government by the dead. On this subject, Lafcadio Hearn writes: ''. . . not only government, but almost everything in Japanese society, derives directly or indirectly from this ancestor cult; and in all matters, the dead, rather than the living have been the rulers of the nation and the shapers of its destiny . . .''[55]

What is normally called ancestor worship or *manes* worship appears to be common to all traditional societies (though the term 'worship' is not strictly correct, the relationship being more informal than this would suggest). It is not a cult by itself, but forms an important part of the total relationship between man and the supernatural, whose nature we have already examined. If the cult of man's direct ancestors play a greater part in his life than any other cult, it is because of the singular importance of the family unit, around which centres the vast proportion of his daily

* See 'Science and Social Control' p.70.

38

concerns.

Tyler writes: "The dead ancestor, now passed into a deity, simply goes on protecting his own family and receiving suit and service from them as of old; the dead chief still watches over his own tribe, still holds his authority by helping friends and harming enemies, still rewards the right and sharply punishes the wrong."[56]

Lafcadio Hearn considers that the following beliefs ". . . underlie all forms of persistent ancestor worship in all climes and countries:

"I — The dead remain in this world — haunting their tombs, and also their former homes, and sharing invisibly in the life of their living descendants.

"II — All the dead become gods, in the sense of acquiring supernatural power; but they retain the characters which distinguished them during life.

"III — The happiness of the dead depends upon the respectful service rendered them by the living; and the happiness of the living depends upon the fulfilment of pious duty to the dead."[55]

## Fear of Death

In a traditional society, a man views his own life as but a link in an infinite chain of being. When he dies, he will live on as an ancestral spirit — which means no more than graduating to a superior and more prestigious age-grade — and in this form he will continue as a member of his family and his community. Even when dead, he will remain in touch with his loved ones, whom he will continue to serve and who will continue to serve him. Hence, he does not entertain our pathological fear of death, and he would find it difficult to understand the logic of heart transplants, for instance, or of subjecting the moribund to appalling torture in our factory-like hospitals, so as to prolong their lives for a few more agonising weeks.

At the same time, the notion of paradise is totally foreign to him. To be consigned to such a place would mean breaking away from his family and his community, a thought which, rather than provide him with succour, would fill him with the deepest despair.

It is for this reason that there is little mention of a future life in the Old Testament. The notion only appears in later Judaism, after the triumph of the priests of Jahweh over the practitioners of the old tribal religion with its ancestral cult and associated beliefs and practices. Thus Lods writes: "It was not till about the second century B.C. that Jahwism, having destroyed the old animistic belief in survival as a false and dangerous superstition, actually replaced the consolations, gloomy at best, which it offered, by a new hope, namely that of a resurrection or immortality accompanied by judgment after death. Hence Jahwism presents the phenomenon, somewhat disconcerting to our modern ideas, of a religion in which the belief in a future life for the individual was long an alien and unwelcome element.''[40]

## The Social Structure of the Gods

As already mentioned, the cult of the ancestors is not merely a family affair, but will be practised at all the other levels of social organisation. Thus Lafcadio Hearn writes of Japan: "The three forms of the Shinto worship of ancestors are the Domestic Cult, the Communal Cult and the State Cult; or, in other words, the worship of family ancestors, the worship of clan or tribal ancestors and the worship of imperial ancestors. The first is the religion of the home; the second is the religion of the local divinity, or titular god; the third is the national religion.''[55]

This appears to be the case in all traditional societies. Driver shows how the differences in the organisation of the gods among North American Indian societies could be explained in terms of their differing social structures: "There was a strong tendency to arrange gods in a ranked hierarchy in areas where people were ranked in a similar manner, and to ignore such ranking where egalitarianism dominated human societies. Thus the people of Meso-America carefully ranked their gods, while those in the Sub-Arctic Plateau and Great Basin believed in large numbers of spirits of about equal rank. Other areas tended to be intermediate in this respect. Among the Pueblos where many spiritual personalities were widely recognised to be designated as gods, there was little tendency towards ranking, just as there was more equality among human beings.''[57]

The people of Alor, as described by Cora Dubois, have a very loosely organised society. Few constraints are applied at a level higher than that of the family, and the family itself is very weak. The average Alorese is undisciplined and self-indulgent, and has little regard for authority of any kind. Their pantheon appears to reflect this social organisation very closely: "They have a culture hero and a supreme deity, but these play a very small part in their thought. Ancestral spirits are more important, but behaviour to them is loose and undisciplined, just as it is towards their parents . . . The dead are merely pressing and insistent predators who can enforce their demands through supernatural powers. This is precisely the experience of the child with his parents. Hence, he obeys reluctantly and grudgingly.''[58]

The Manus, a small nation of traders and fishermen, serve as another example of a loosely organised people who likewise regard their gods as loosely organised. According to Goode, their religious system ". . . is highly individualistic, in that the sacred entity worshipped is the spirit of one person, usually the father . . .''[59]

40

The Swazi have developed a cohesive and hierarchically organised society, and, according to Hilda Kuper, their gods are organised in exactly the same way: "In the ancestral cult, the world of the living is projected onto a world of spirit (*emadloti*). Men and women, old and young, aristocrats and commoners, continue the patterns of superiority and inferiority established by earthly experiences. Paternal and maternal spirits exercise complementary roles, similar to those operating in daily life on earth; the paternal role re-inforces legal and economic obligations; the maternal exercises a less formalised protective influence. Although the cult is set in a kinship framework, it is extended to the nation through the king, who is regarded as the father of all Swazi. His ancestors are the most powerful of all the spirits."[60]

In Dahomey, a centralised kingdom was developed at an early stage. According to Herskovits: ". . . the organisation of the Dahomean gods is a reflection of the organisation of the society, though in a somewhat rough fashion. They include the idea of reigning over a kingdom, and of a hierarchy of organisation influencing all aspects of the social and economic life."[61]

## The Changing Structure of the Gods

It is interesting to trace changes in the organisation of the gods following important social changes.

Robertson Smith[45] shows how, with the breakdown of tribal society during the beginning of the historical period, social structures underwent considerable change. The course of change in Greece and Rome, however, was very different from that in the East. In the West, the aristocracy managed to gain power at the expense of the kings, whereas in Asia the kings held their own until their states were eventually destroyed by larger and more powerful neighbours.

Robertson Smith points out that: "This diversity of political fortune is reflected in the diversity of religious development. For as the national god did not at first supersede tribal and family deities any more than the king superseded tribal and family institutions, the tendency of the West, where the kingship succumbed, was towards a divine aristocracy of many gods, only modified by a weak reminiscence of the old kingship in the not very effective sovereignty of Zeus, while in the East the national god tended to acquire a really monarchic sway."[45]

What is particularly significant is that our concept of monotheism has come to us from the East. Although the idea of a universal god is an old one, in tribal society it played only a very small part in people's pre-occupations. No cult was associated with the universal god, and he was addressed only on very rare occasions, not by the individual but by the tribe as a whole.

Cullen Young,[62] who was a missionary in Africa for 27 years, observes that tribal Africans scarcely ever refer to god. The reason, of course, is that tribal man has no need of a universal god: he looks for guidance in his day-to-day problems to the ancestral spirits, who are less remote, and he has no conception of a universal society such as might require a universal god for its protection and sanctification.

Cullen Young writes that: "The non-African intruder within this strange thought-world is not culpably guilty, however, of error when he concludes that the idea of God seems absent. He is, for the time being, moving within a sphere where reference to God is simply not required. He will find it not easy to discover any point or moment in African communal living at which the belief in the continuing presence and active power of those whom we describe as 'dead' is not sufficient in itself for confidence and trust."[62]

However, it is easy to see how a national god can slowly evolve into a universal one. This is undoubtedly what happened in the case of Jahweh. He probably started off as the Thunder God of the Kennites, a Bedouin tribe of the Sinai peninsula, with whom the Jews came into contact during their sojourn in the desert. He then became the national god of the southern Jews, and only briefly the national god of the precarious Jewish kingdom resulting from the temporary fusion of Judah and Israel under David and Solomon. It is only with St. Paul that he became a universal god.

As Robertson Smith writes: "What is often described as the natural tendency of Semitic religion towards ethical monotheism, is in the main nothing more than a consequence of the alliance of religion with monarchy."[45]

## The Classification of the Natural Environment

Tribal man is able to establish his relationship with his natural environment in such a way that it is not treated simply as a resource for the satisfaction of his short-term needs. The natural environment is classified in terms of the same classificatory system that accommodates his society, his ancestors, and his gods.

Different animals are associated with each different clan, and are invested with some sort of *mana*, or vital force, which renders them sacred to it. Other animals are sacred to the tribe as a whole, the degree of sacredness varying from one animal to another.

In this way, the natural environment is sanctified, and a complete set of ritualised relationships is established between a traditional society and the forms of life with which it is in contact. As a result of these relationships, Radcliffe Brown points out: "Each group is responsible for the ritual care of a certain number of species as a result of which the maintenance of that group is believed to be assured. For the tribe all these species are of importance, and the ceremonies are thus a sort of cooperative effort, involving a division of labour, by which the normal processes of nature and the supply of food are provided for.''[29]

*It is by desanctifying his environment that modern man has been able so systematically to destroy it and by sanctifying himself that he has rationalised this destruction.*

## The Dynamic Principle

We have seen that the religio-culture of traditional man constitutes a complete, four-dimensional model of his relationship to his family, his society, and his environment, in which he sees the whole thing as one vast continuum.

This model enables a traditional society to mediate a single, integrated pattern of responses. A modern industrial state, on the other hand, must rely on the information provided by science, and as a result its pattern of behaviour is nothing more than a patchwork of expedients, for science, committed to the reductionist method and divided into a host of watertight disciplines each with a distinct methodology and terminology, is unable to provide an integrated pattern of information.*

It is not enough for a religio-culture to supply a model of the society's relationship with its environment; to ensure that the society can *maintain* this relationship it must provide a dynamic principle — a goal structure and a set of rules for achieving those goals.

At the level of the family unit, this presents no problem. As Malinowski has pointed out, man is, genetically at least, a family animal.[21] Unless the family is seriously interfered with (as is the case in industrial societies), the various members of a family unit will fulfil their appropriate functions in it without reluctance.

A man obtains the greatest satisfaction by behaving in a husbandly manner towards his wife and in a fatherly manner towards his children, while a woman obtains the greatest satisfaction by fulfilling her functions as a wife and mother, and later as a grandmother. *It happens that, by behaving in the way that ensures the maximum personal satisfaction for themselves, a man and a woman at the same time contribute to the stability of the family unit.*[63] This is precisely the relationship obtaining in any natural system between the parts and the whole, and provides the dynamic principle required to ensure stability at the level of the family.†

A society, however, is a more precarious system. The bonds that hold it

* See Chapter 4 'Science and Social Control'.

† This is an illustration of the Hierarchical Cooperation Principle. See Chapter 1 'Society as a Natural System', p.9.

together are culturally determined, and, as Malinowski has shown,[21] are basically extensions of those which hold together the family — hence the elaborate kinship terminology used to classify members of the social group, most of whom are outside the basic family unit.

In this case, the motivation that is exploited is the quest for prestige, which was probably originally associated with man's desire to shine in the eyes of the woman of his choice and to compete with other men for her favours.

### Prestige

It is one of the tenets of our industrial society that man's overriding goal is to maximise his material benefits. This, like so many of the governing assumptions of industrial society, is based on a superficial examination of the behaviour of man during only a minute fraction of his total experience. A study of the behaviour of traditional societies reveals that man, in normal conditions, is culturally a social rather than an economic animal.

As Polanyi writes: "The outstanding discovery of recent historical research is that man's economy, as a rule, is submerged in his social relationships. He does not act so as to safeguard his individual interest in the possession of material goods; he acts so as to safeguard his social standing, his social claims, his social assets. He values material goods only in so far as they serve this end. Neither the process of production nor that of distribution is linked to specific economic interests attached to the possession of goods; but every single step in that process is geared to a number of special interests which eventually ensure that the required step be taken. These interests will be very different in a small hunting or fishing community from those in a vast despotic society, but in either case the economic system will be run on non-economic motives."[64]

As Tarde puts it: "Primitive man is not a miser, nor a sage, nor a beast of prey . . . but a peacock."[65]

Linton pointed out how this desire for prestige is used in traditional societies as an instrument of control: "The human desire for prestige is probably the most useful of all the innate qualities of man. The hope of gaining prestige, or the fear of losing it, does more than anything else to hold the average individual to the proper performance of his role."[32]

How is this desire for prestige exploited by society? The answer is that, in the world-view of a society, prestige is achieved by the fulfilment of precisely those functions that will enable a society to survive. Thus, in a fishing society, prestige will be associated with proficiency in catching fish; among hunter gatherers, prestige is associated with success in the hunt; in a society geared to warlike pursuits it is the successful warrior who will be the most admired.

To become a successful fisherman, hunter or warrior, however, the acquisition of the necessary skills is not sufficient. It is necessary to accumulate vital force, or *mana* as it is known amongst the Polynesians. We have already mentioned this vital force, possession of which by individuals, animals, or even objects confers upon them an aura of sacredness. This notion is closely associated with that of god, and, according to Lods, it may well be that ". . . the very ancient term which is found in all Semitic languages to express the idea of 'god' under the various forms of *el* (Hebrew), *ilu* (Babylonian), *ilah* (Arab) originally denoted the vague force which is the source of all strength and life, the divine rather than a god or divine personality: it would have had a meaning similar to that of the term *mana* among the Polynesians, the Indian *brahman*, and the Latin *numen*."[40]

In Africa this vital force is referred to as *muntu* among the Baluba, *nyama* among the Dogom, and *megbe* by the Congo pygmies.

The notion that power can be acquired or lost, increased or decreased in accordance with a carefully formulated set of rules appears to be common to most traditional societies. The principle is referred to as 'dynamism'.

Driberg regards this notion as underlying the religious beliefs and philosophy of traditional societies throughout Africa. He writes: "This spiritual force consists of an abstract power or natural potency, all-pervasive and definitely never regarded anthropomorphically."[66]

Father Placide Tempels in his study of Bantu philosophy writes: "Vital force is the central theme of Bantu philosophy. The goal of all efforts among the Bantu can only be to intensify this vital force. One can only understand their customs if one interprets them as a means of preserving or increasing one's stock of vital force. It is the only ideal he is willing to suffer or sacrifice himself for."[67]

All illnesses, depressions, failures in any field of activity are taken as a reduction in this vital force and can be avoided only by maintaining one's stock of it. When a Baluba prays, it is to obtain from the ancestral spirits or other deities an increase in *muntu*. The rituals he performs are designed to increase this vital force. Those performed at birth, circumcision, marriage, etc., involve such important increases that, on each occasion, new names are acquired, corresponding to the type of *muntu* thereby obtained. Each time, the old name must no longer be pronounced, for fear of reducing his *muntu*.

Taboos are observed for the same reason. Transgression always involves a reduction of *muntu*, to an extent which depends on the importance of the taboo. Everyday interpersonal relations also provide an opportunity for increasing or decreasing *muntu*. A powerful man is described as a *muntu mukulumpe*, a man with a great deal of *muntu*, whereas a man of no social significance is referred to as a *muntu mutupu*, or one who has but a small amount of *muntu*. A complex vocabulary is used to describe all the changes that can affect one's stock of *muntu*. The verbs *kufwa* and *kufwididila* indicate degrees of loss of vital force. A man with none left at all is known as a *mufu*. He is as good as dead.

Schebesta describes the idea of *megbe* as it is understood by the pygmies of the Ituri forests. "*Megbe* is spread out everywhere, but its power does not manifest itself everywhere with the same force nor in the same way. Certain animals are richly endowed with it. Humans possess a lot more of some types of *megbe* but less of other types. Able men are precisely those who have accumulated a lot of *megbe*, this is true of witch-doctors"[68] (author's translation).

Kardiner explains the behaviour pattern of the Comanche Indians in the same way. They appear to have: ". . . the most ingenious concept of 'power' which can be borrowed, lent, pooled and freely dispersed among the entire group."[69]

Their behaviour provides an idea of how vital force is used to achieve the stable relationship of a society with its environment. According to Kardiner, they regard all the constituents of the environment as possessing some sort of power.[69] The greatest is personified by the eagle, the earth, the sky and the sun. The highest force is God. After him come the first fathers who founded various clans, and next comes the head of the tribe; the living also form a hierarchy in accordance with their vital power. Animals, plants and minerals are organised in the same way. However, since their role is to satisfy the need of the humans, they have less vital power. Sorcerers and witches are considered to be capable of manipulating vital power in people and objects, to the detriment and death of their fellows.

In accordance with tribal custom: ". . . certain things can be done, certain words spoken, certain thoughts harboured . . . and to break these taboos involves releasing hidden forces, with the consequent destruction of vital force for the transgressor." It was through the mediation of this power that the breaking of taboos was punished. A complicated set of rules governed the transfer of vital power from one person or object to another.

The sky power could not be transferred to men. Earth power could only be transferred to those who had miraculously recovered from wounds. Next came the power of the eagle, and the various lesser powers, each of which provided its possessor with certain specific benefits. Thus bear power conferred invulnerability; the burrowing owl gave the power of being hard to hit; beavers and buffaloes gave the power of the rapid healing of wounds; the mountain lion gave tremendous strength; the snake the ability to recover from the bite of snakes; the meadow lark the power to 'go directly home'. Minnow power acted as a love charm. The horse, dog and coyote were associated with no specific powers. Success in hunting was attributed to the power conferred by 'tiny black men with invisible arrows'.

The possession of power was double-edged, in the sense that its possession subjected one to corresponding taboos, whose violation automatically reduced the power involved. It appears that all Comanche ritual could be explained in terms of obtaining, getting rid of, increasing, or reducing all those different powers. Thus a specific ritual permitted middle-aged men to get rid of warrior powers in order to free themselves from the corresponding taboos, which were growing increasingly irksome. Other rituals, such as the sun ceremony, had the object of obtaining specific powers from the medicine-man in charge.[69]

### Centralisation of Vital Force

As one would expect, the amount of vital force residing at the different levels of social organisation reflects the society's social structure. In a very loose society such as that of the people of Alor, one would expect individuals and families to be endowed with a considerable proportion of the society's vital force. On the other hand, in a highly centralised society, a traditional kingdom such as ancient Egypt, Dahomey, or Benin in West Africa, the vital force becomes concentrated in the person of the divine king, who is in fact divine precisely for this reason. In such a society, the welfare of all the inhabitants is regarded as totally dependent on the fulfilment of certain rituals designed to preserve and increase the king's stock of vital force, and on the observance of the many taboos surrounding his person.

That this was true of the ancient Hellenic kingdom is apparent from Homer, who writes: ''When a blameless and god-fearing king maintains impartial justice, the brown earth is rich in corn and in barley, and the trees are laden with fruit; the ewes constantly bring forth young, the seas abound in fishes, there is nothing that does not prosper when there is good government and the people are happy.''[70]

The practice of killing the king at regular intervals, described by Frazer in *The Golden Bough*,[50] makes much sense — it implies that he had ceased to be a fit repository for the vital force of the society. In terms of the world-view of the society concerned, the society's stock of vital force could only be renewed by transferring it to someone else, who must thereby be crowned in his stead. As is generally known, in some kingdoms the king was ritually murdered at the end of each year, a custom incomprehensible to those not aware of the specific law governing the transfer of vital force in such societies.

Equally incomprehensible would be the custom of putting to death commoners who have trodden in the king's shadow or committed some other ritual offence, if it were not realised that in terms of the society's world-view this misdemeanour could lead to terrible social calamities.

## Universalism

As a society disintegrates, its citizens lose interest in its affairs and there is little left to differentiate them from the rest of humanity.

Hammond relates the development of universalism in the Greek City State as reflected in the teachings of its philosophers to the increasing withdrawal from social affairs.[71] Plato withdrew with his pupils to the Grove of the hero Academus in the Attic countryside; and thereafter his Academy became cut off from real life and devoted to the study of pure mathematics and other intellectual pursuits. Similarly, Epicurus established his school in a garden outside Athens. The garden became a symbol of retirement from the world into a pleasant existence, such as the gods led in their remote heaven.

The Stoics made a gallant attempt to resist this trend. The City State had disintegrated, however, and the Stoics chose to adopt a broader concept of citizenship. They considered that the true social reality was the inhabited world, *oecumene*, and preached that man owed a duty to this illusory entity. Rather than retreat from society, Zeno and his disciples stood in the painted Stoa, a public colonnade in the centre of Athens, and addressed all who would listen. Their message was world citizenship and the universal brotherhood of man, the same fiction that we are taught today. Needless to say, it failed.

Hammond writes: "Stoicism offered a solution at once practical and noble to the problem of the relation of the individual to the State in the new monarchies . . . Yet, this solution was not wholly satisfactory because it was one-sided. It placed on the individual a duty toward his fellow men but it offered him no corresponding privilege, such as citizenship had constituted in the City State."[71]

*The same forces which made man entertain the notion of the universal brotherhood of man made him direct his thought towards a universal god.*

The development of universalism is traced by Robertson Smith.[45] Among the pre-Islamic Arabs, as the tribes disintegrated and the old tribal gods lost their function, no permanent kingdom established itself. This meant that there was no powerful local god to whom allegiance could be transferred and so, to secure the satisfaction and the succour previously provided by the tribal gods, it became the practice to worship gods in some distant holy place, and to go on pilgrimage to their shrine. As Robertson Smith writes, the pilgrims ". . . were the guests of the god, and were received as such by the inhabitants of the holy places. They approached the god as strangers, not with the old joyous confidence of

48

national worship, but with atoning ceremonies and rites of self-mortification, and their acts of worship were carefully prescribed for them by qualified instructors, the prototypes of the modern Meccan *motan wif*. The progress of heathenism towards universalism, as it is displayed in these usages, seemed only to widen the gulf between deity and man, to destroy the naive trustfulness of the old religion without substituting a better way for man to be at one with his god, to weaken the moral ideas of nationality without bringing in a higher morality of universal obligation.''[45]

It is also interesting to trace changes in the organisation of the gods of Ancient Egypt in terms of the changes in their social organisation. According to Wallace Budge, the original religion of the Ancient Egyptians was ancestor worship.[72] They had a vague belief in a universal god who was regarded as the creator or moulder, as is the case among surviving tribal societies today, but this god, Pautti, was regarded as too far removed from the world of men to concern himself with their affairs. Significantly, it was not he who was destined to become the god of the later Egyptian empires.

The original tribal societies of Ancient Egypt disappeared during the historical period and we find emerging the two kingdoms of Upper and Lower Egypt, which always remained distinct and tended to preserve their independence in times of trouble. These were divided up into Nomes, which were linked together in a sort of federal system. In the course of time, the federal system became progressively more centralised and the power of the Nomes was correspondingly reduced. Social structures were further eroded during the long period of foreign domination by the Assyrians, Persians, and Greeks, until eventually the Egyptian people were transformed into something which approximates to our contemporary concept of a nation: a structureless mass society.

These changes were accompanied by a corresponding change in the structure of the gods. During the Middle Empire, the fusion of the two national gods Amon and Ra occurred. The tendency towards the fusion of the gods became even greater during the time of troubles preceding the Saite renaissance, and the process continued until the Ptolemaic period, by which time all the male gods had fused into the person of Osiris, and all the female gods into that of Isis.[72]

Since there was no longer any social structure, there was no longer any basis for structuring the pantheon, which disintegrated. This left only the supreme god at the top of a defunct hierarchy, but now he acquired a wife and child, which the supreme god of a tribal society does not possess.

We recall that in a tribal society the supreme god is not part of the social scheme of things, whereas all the other gods are, as members of an extended family, clan, tribe, or ethnic group. Under the changed conditions, however, these social structures are defunct. The only social unit to survive is the nuclear family, and, accordingly, a nuclear family is attributed to the supreme god.

Erich Fromm has argued that the worship of father and mother gods (and indeed child and grandmother gods) satisfies different needs.[28] Worship of a mother figure is associated with the need for a mother's love. This, in sharp contrast to a father's love, is relatively unconditional. The child can behave in the most atrocious manner without seriously affecting the love its mother displays towards it. A father's love, on the contrary, must be earned: it is conferred for behaviour conforming to the father's ethical code, which, in a stable society, will coincide with that of his society. As a grandmother has no responsibility for disciplining the child, her love is even more unconditional than the mother's.

Societies which have worshipped a mother figure have tended to be self-indulgent. Puritanical societies, in which virtue is associated with rigorous observance of a code of ethics, will worship a father figure.

This tendency could not be better illustrated than by the social circumstances that in ancient Egypt governed the rise of the cult of Isis and the corresponding decline of the cult of Osiris, and in Christendom the development of the cult of the Virgin Mary beginning in the anomie of the 7th century and its abandonment by the 'revitalisation' movements that culminated in the Reformation.

In these conditions, a society's structure ceases to be sanctified by its pantheon. It is thereby deprived of the very basis of its stability.

### Vital Force in a Disintegrating Society

With the disintegration of a society and the destruction of its cultural pattern, the functioning of the dynamic principle is equally affected. However, in our aberrant industrial society, the notion of vital force has not been entirely lost. Although we no longer believe in God or gods, we do believe that science, technology, and industry will create for us a material paradise here on Earth, and undoubtedly we attribute a kind of supernatural power to the scientific knowledge that can bring this about. The possession of scientific knowledge is regarded as the key to success, a passport to status and riches. Money likewise is imbued with vital force, since it sustains the technological development and the industrial enterprises which exploit this scientific knowledge.

This notion of vital force, however, no longer provides our society with a goal structure enabling it to achieve a stable relationship with its environment. Instead it drives society towards ever greater discontinuities.

### Otherworldliness

As a society disintegrates, it constitutes an ever less satisfactory environment. A man is no longer surrounded by a set of his fellows, each of whom is in a different relationship with him, from each of whom he can expect different services, and to whom he has different customary obligations. Instead he is embedded in an anonymous mass of undifferentiated humanity, from which he feels increasingly alienated. At the same time his gods are becoming correspondingly more human, and *he transfers to them the duties that previously he owed to his fellow men.* Whenever this process occurs, there gradually grows up a body of specialists to exploit man's growing preoccupation with the gods. Religion is institutionalised; the priesthood grows in size and influence; and the means of serving the gods become divorced from the means of serving man.

There are accompanying changes both in ethical values and in the determinants of prestige. In order to be admired, it becomes necessary to achieve goals very different from those which would evoke the admiration of a traditional society. These changes proceed by positive feedback, in that they lead to the further disintegration of society, and hence to further changes in the determinants of prestige, and so on. Lecky writes: "the first idea which the phrase 'a very good man' would have suggested to an early Roman would probably have been that of great and distinguished patriotism, and the passion and interest of such a man in his country's cause were in direct proportion to his moral elevation. Ascetic Christianity decisively diverted moral enthusiasm into another channel, and the civic virtues, in consequence, necessarily declined."[74]

'Otherworldliness' became even more pronounced in the religio-culture of many of the medieval heresies, such as those of the Bogomiles and Cathars, who tended to regard the world as being so evil that it could only have been the creation of the devil. In such conditions, the only behaviour that could conceivably meet with God's approval was to divorce oneself entirely from the concerns of this world and preoccupy oneself exclusively with those of the next.

Clearly, no psychological terrain could have been less propitious for the emergence of our modern technological society. Not so, however, for that furnished by later non-conformist heresies. The Puritans reacted against 'otherworldliness' and sought to reintroduce duties towards men, not as a substitute for duties towards God but as the only true means of serving him. To achieve the Christian Paradise it was no longer sufficient to fulfil empty rituals; people must submit to a rigid set of behavioural constraints which banished frivolities and put a premium on hard work. Work was thereby equated with virtue and the materially successful with the righteous.

It is the well known thesis of Weber that it was only among men who had developed so singular a world-view, who in fact, went so far as to regard technology not only as a tool for ensuring one's own personal comfort but also for achieving one's peace with God, that the Industrial Revolution could conceivably have occurred.

Possibly, the process had a positive feedback component in that the new industrial classes had a strong psychological stake in a philosophy which provided a perfect justification for their activities, which enabled them by the same efforts, in fact, to serve both God and Mammon.

As industrial activities began to spread throughout what are now the industrialised societies, so did the ethic underlying and justifying them itself undergo a corresponding change. Preoccupation with the *material* products of industry began to obscure their ethical justification, and the materialist paradise which science, technology and industry appeared to be creating came to replace its conventional Christian equivalent, which to practical men, appeared ever more remote and speculative.

In this way, perhaps, can be traced the genesis of the goal structure of technological man: the achievement of a materialist paradise in which drudgery, poverty, social inequality, ignorance, unemployment, famine, disease, and even death (i.e. what are assumed to be the ills with which man has always been afflicted) will have been eliminated once and for all.

Needless to say, such a paradise can never be achieved, for to do so would mean violating most of the basic laws which our scientists have themselves formulated. To move in this direction, however, must mean systematically increasing the impact of human activities on biological, ecological and social systems and thereby correspondingly increasing overall instability. Unless the aberrant religio-culture which provides the rationale for this fatal process is shattered, it must eventually lead to the destruction of our environment and the extinction of the human species.

## The Redevelopment of Social Religion

Christianity has not always been a force causing men to be detached from their duties towards their society. In rural areas of Europe, veneration of local saints has provided communities with a sense of identity and purpose.

In the case of the Medieval cities of Southern Europe at least, the cult of patron saints such as St. Mark in Venice, St. Catharine in Siena, and St. Spiros in Corfu was often more developed than that of God himself or of the Virgin Mary. This coincided with the development of a powerful sense of patriotism and social obligations often reminiscent of the City States of antiquity. This tendency is likely to recur today.

As industrial society disintegrates, we may expect that out of the accompanying chaos there will arise a growing number of Messianic movements which will attempt to establish a new social order based upon a new view of man's relationship with his environment. Many of these will adopt at least a facade of Christianity, re-interpreting the Gospels to provide the religio-cultural rationale for the stable societies of the future.

# 4 Science and Social Control

We live in an Age of Faith, not in God but in science. If most of us are still capable of facing the mounting problems of the world today with relative equanimity, it is because we sincerely believe that science will provide us with the means of solving them, just as we would have expected God to do were we living half a millenium earlier.

Our scientists are functionally the priests of our industrial society. It is only they who are capable of mobilising, for our purposes, the limitless powers of science, of acting thereby as the intermediaries in our relationship with this new and formidable deity.

It is not surprising that their writings are imbued with an aura of sanctity previously reserved for the holy texts of the established religions. If a proposition is classified as 'scientific', then it must be true, indeed incontestable. If, on the other hand, something is branded as 'unscientific' then it must be the work of a charlatan. This has provided the scientific establishment with the power to prevent any undesired deviation from scientific orthodoxy, just as, in the same way, the Catholic establishment of the Middle Ages would excommunicate any heretic whose teachings were a challenge to their authority.

Indeed, one finds among the annals of the scientific world some which are strangely reminiscent of Medieval witch-hunts. Consider, for instance, the response of the scientific establishment to the publication of *Limits to Growth*.[76] It was branded as unscientific by both *Nature* and *Science*, the world's two most prestigious scientific journals.

In Britain the inquisition was led by Lord Zuckerman, once chief scientist to the British Government. It is easy to see how he exploited the terms 'scientific' and 'unscientific' to discredit this very important work in the following outburst in a speech delivered in Stockholm during the 1972 United Nations Conference on the Human Environment: "Our newspapers," he proclaimed, "urged on by a plethora of *pseudo-scientific* books, articles and speeches are filled with items which warn us that irreversible damage is beind done to our physical environment . . . I have referred to a book *Limits to Growth* which has been hailed . . . mainly by the *scientifically* uninitiated as a *scientific* statement about man's environmental problems . . . for my part I have no hesitation in saying that I am among those professional students of environmental problems who dismiss the book as *unscientific* nonsense.'"[77]

## What is Science?

In view of this, it is clearly important that one should know just what 'science' is, and precisely how one determines what constitutes a 'scientific' proposition.

'Science' does not appear to have ever been adequately defined. In general, it seems to involve the accumulation of knowledge. But what is knowledge? Here we encounter a major snag: to answer this question we must leave what is generally regarded as the realm of 'exact science', and enter that of epistemology or the theory of knowledge.

However, for scientists to regard epistemology as being outside the scope of science is to renounce the responsibility for examing the assumptions on which their work is based, that is, for determining to what extent it is justified.

This task is delegated to people who work outside the field of science and know very little about it, and who, like most specialists today, tend to regard their field of study as largely autonomous, i.e. as something that can be studied in isolation from everything else. As a result, one finds little in current epistemological writings that can serve to provide a theoretical basis for modern science — a lamentable situation. As Einstein wrote: "Epistemology without contact with science becomes an empty scheme, science without epistemology — in so far as it is thinkable at all — primitive and muddled."

## What is Knowledge?

Knowledge is clearly some sort of information. To qualify as knowledge, however, this information must display certain characteristics. According to Ayer, who appears to be one of the principal spokesmen for the modern school of empiricism, it must be true, we must know it to be true, and for the right reasons. This implies, above all, that knowledge is conscious information of some sort. This is presumably the only type of information that can be studied empirically. Also, it is by basing one's behaviour exclusively on such information that one is regarded as acting 'rationally'.

If epistemologists knew a little about such subjects as cybernetics, ethology and psychology, they would realise that conscious information

54

plays by no means a determining role in the behaviour of even the most sophisticated members of the species *Homo rapiens*. To understand the use of conscious information without reference to that of unconscious information is simply not possible. In fact to understand the use of information in the brain is difficult without examining it as part of a general theory of information, which must mean examining the way it is built up and made use of by systems at all levels of organisation. Such a study would reveal that information in the brain is built up and used in very much the same way as it is in a gene-pool or a fertilised egg and that there is in fact only one way of organising and using information among natural systems.

### Control

The reason for this is that information is built up *for one purpose only*, and that is *to constitute a model of the relationship between the system of which it is part and its particular environment.* Information is, in fact, of no value by itself as a basis for behaviour. To identify a technological device as being a nuclear power station, for instance, is of no value if one has not previously built up a model of the relationship between a nuclear power station, the biosphere of which we are a part, and the rest of the technosphere of which it is part. Only in this way can one understand what are its implications and hence how we should react towards these diabolical contrivances. It is a serious illusion to suppose that the mere fact of attaching a label to something provides information about it.

*If information is only organised for a single purpose, this is also true of the model of which it is part. A model is only built up for the purpose of serving as a basis for the control of a system's behaviour towards its environment.*

This whole notion of control is largely ignored by epistemologists as well as many scientists who have implicitly adopted the empiricist position. There is a good reason for this, of course. If a system is controlled, this must mean that it is goal-directed or purposive, for what else can control mean but to keep something on its correct course? And how can it be kept on its correct course if it doesn't have one? The goal, needless to say, cannot be pin-pointed in space-time. It is simply that course along which discontinuities and their corrections are reduced to a minimum. By taking such a course a system is capable of maintaining its basic structure in the face of environmental challenges, i.e. *of remaining stable.*

It is also by taking such a course that free energy is reduced to a minimum *over a long period.* In this way the system remains in four-dimensional equilibrium with its environment. *This principle of directiveness is irreconcilable with empiricist philosophy*, since it cannot be induced on the basis of observation, i.e. according to what empiricists regard as the only legitimate method for building up knowledge. Also, it justifies a methodology for building up knowledge which is in competition with induction. I refer to deduction from the general principle cited. Thus one could postulate that to maintain its stability in specific environmental conditions a system must be able to achieve a given set of sub-goals, those that, in the circumstances, enable it to maintain its stability. A specific behavioural act could therefore be explained in terms of its contribution to the achievement of a sub-goal, and judged in accordance with its ability to do so. This is, in fact, the cybernetic as opposed to the reductionist approach.

To reject the directivity principle, however, is to reject the very principle of organising information, and hence, among other things, the possibility of science. The reason for this is very simple. Information is built up out of data, the raw materials of information. Data, as we shall see, are interpreted in the light of a system's model of its relationship with its environment. They then constitute information. This means putting order into what might previously have appeared to be random data. This is only adaptive if this order corresponds to something, i.e. if it reflects an ordered situation. Since behaviour is, by its very nature, dynamic, i.e. involves change, this change must be orderly, *which means that it must be heading in a given direction* (see Appendix II).

## The Mechanism of Control

Cybernetics has probably contributed more than any other discipline to the unification of science by demonstrating that control, at all levels of organisation, is achieved in the same way — that, in fact, the basic cybernetic model is of universal application.

Data are obtained, transduced and interpreted. A hypothesis or model is postulated and projected back onto the data, followed by a modified hypothesis and a further projection. Each time the hypothesis is made to fit better with the general model of the system — by modifying either the hypothesis or the general model. This can be repeated over and over again, and in this way there will be a continual monitoring of a series of ever better hypotheses formulated after successive accretions of information. This process gives rise to a damped system, i.e. one in which errors are progressively reduced. If behaviour is taken as tending towards a position of four-dimensional equilibrium, i.e. along an equilibrium course, which we can represent by a straight line, it will in fact take the form of a series of oscillations of ever-diminishing size — tending towards the reduction of errors, and associated with the development of an ever better representation of the system. On the other hand, if this mechanism does not function properly, i.e. if the system gets out of control, then the oscillations will increase in size. This of course cannot continue indefinitely; the discontinuities would eventually become insupportable and the system would collapse — just as is happening to our society today.

At this point it might be worth noting that, for two million years or so, human social systems displayed considerable stability. Unstable social systems appear to have been largely confined to recent times, i.e. to the period following the neolithic revolution.[11] Even during this period, traditional societies which have succeeded in remaining outside the orbit of mainstream civilisations have continued to display considerable stability. Such stability can only be achieved in one way, and that is by the operation of a control mechanism of the type described above.

This mechanism is a society's culture, of which an essential component is a specific world-view, comprising a model of the society's relationship with its environment, a corresponding goal-structure, and a means of achieving it.[78]

Science appears to be an attempt to replace the cultural information embodied in traditional world-views, that is, information which is very different in the case of each traditional society, by means of a single organisation of information, which should theoretically serve *each of them equally well. It is an attempt, in fact, to substitute objective for subjective information as a basis for control.*

Such a substitution has many implications, which I shall look into later. First of all let us consider what can conceivably justify it.

Epistemologically, the answer is fairly obvious. Traditional information does not qualify as 'knowledge'. It is only true *vis-à-vis* a largely subconscious and very subjective model and not *vis-à-vis* a conscious objective one.

It involves reference to such things as gods and spirits whose presence is empirically unverifiable, and it establishes a strange set of cause-and-effect relationships between man's ritual activities, the behaviour of these gods and spirits, and day-to-day biological, social, and ecological events, a procedure which is regarded as 'irrational'.

If cultural information is organised subjectively, it is assumed that it must provide a society with a very restricted view of its environment, only that which it has so far required for its own specific adaptive purposes. If information be organised objectively, on the other hand, then it will provide a faithful reproduction of the outside world, which should serve as the basis for a much wider range of adaptations, enabling a society, in this way, to adapt to all possible eventualities.

For this to be so, at least two conditions must clearly be satisfied. The first is that relevant objective information can actually be obtained by our scientists and organised so as to constitute an effective model of a society's relationship with its environment. The second is that individuals and the societies into which they are organised are actually able to make use of this information to determine their relationship with their environment. In this paper I shall show that neither of these conditions are satisfied and that for the purpose of social control objective information cannot be substituted for the subjective information contained in traditional culture patterns.

## Reductionism

The first obvious reason why scientific knowledge cannot replace traditional cultural knowledge is that science is reductionist. It seeks to understand the behaviour of a complex system by examining its parts in isolation from each other. Unfortunately, this cannot enable one to understand a complex system which is more than the sum of its component parts. This must be so since a system is above all an organisation and its specific character is not only due to its components *but to the way in which they are organised.*

Thus, if it is possible to build up a great diversity of natural systems from a limited number of components, this is due to the extraordinary difference in the behaviour of these components when used in different ways, i.e. when combined in a particular way with other components. In other words, *a system is very much more than the sum of its component parts.* It is for this reason that studying one in isolation from the larger system of which it is part *provides very little information on the way it will behave in any conditions, save the artificial ones of the laboratory in which the study is being conducted, and in which they alone occur.* Indeed, isolated systems do not exist in nature, any more than do phoenixes or unicorns — and this important fact makes nonsense of most scientific research carried out today.

To illustrate this thesis, let us consider why we understand so little of human nutrition. As Ross Hall,[79] one of the few ecologically orientated nutritionists of today has pointed out, the function of a vitamin or of any other nutrient cannot be understood simply from its chemical composition. Its action, like that of all the other constituents of our food is very different in different environments, i.e. when used in a different way. This means that when flour, for instance, is refined and nutrients are lost, their subsequent reintroduction provides no compensation for this loss. *For wholewheat is a system*, which means that it is more than the sum of its component parts, and by enriching the devitalised flour, we do not restore its lost nutritive value.

This may be confirmed by the fact that, though in Canada, practically all the bread sold is enriched with thiamine and iron, a recent study by Nutrition Canada has revealed that a vast majority of Canadians *suffer*

58

*from thiamine and iron deficiency.*

The fact is that, once we have broken down the wholewheat into its constituent parts, we are incapable of putting it together again in the correct way. All the king's horses and all the king's men, as Ross Hall[79] puts it, cannot put Humpty together again, and what is more, *this is true of any natural system which we may have irresponsibly taken apart.* Thus, if one allows a family to disintegrate into its constituent parts, one cannot reconstitute it by forcing its members who have grown up in isolation from each other, to come back and live together again. The basic interrelationships required to hold a family together cannot be easily restored. Still less, of course, can one recreate a biological organism that has disintegrated into its component cells or molecules.

If we cannot reconstitute a natural system once it has disintegrated, nor can we provide a substitute that satisfies both the countless requirements of the smaller systems, which compose it, or of the larger one, of which it is part. *Whatever we introduce in its stead, in fact, can only be expected to satisfy a minimal proportion of these requirements.* A good illustration of this principle is our attempt, as part of the developmental process, to substitute bottled cows' milk for human milk. Needless to say it is always easy to find experts, who, on the basis of a simplistic notion of human nutrition, assure us of its superiority. One reason often given for this is that it has a higher protein content. As Crawford[80] points out, however, a calf needs more protein because, at birth, *it grows more quickly than does a human baby.* Much more important is the fact that cows' milk contains less polyunsaturated fats which are required for building up brain tissue than does human milk — enough in fact to satisfy the requirements of a calf, but not that of a human baby whose brain grows much more quickly. There are a host of other reasons why cows' milk is a poor substitute for human milk. For instance, it contains an almost equal ratio of calcium and phosphorus, which is undesirable for a human baby, who requires more calcium. The level of sodium in cows' milk is too high and may give rise to primary hypertension. The low level of copper in cows' milk has been related to the reduced transportation of iron and hence contributes to the iron deficiency associated with anaemia, which is common among North American infants. In human milk too, the proportion of long chain polyunsaturated fatty acids and short chain fatty acids is that which most favours their absorption and conversion to energy in the human baby.

Other characteristics of human milk also favour the necessary absorption of palmitic acid, which appears not to be the case in cows' milk. The ratio of whey to casein protein is also higher in human milk than in cows' milk, which minimises the amount of nitrogen that must be excreted by the liver and kidneys.

Furthermore, the gastro-intestinal tract of a baby fed on human milk is colonised by the bacteria lactobacillis bifidis. The important role played by this bacillus seems to have been grossly underestimated. Its presence appears to be essential to assure the absorption of protein and other nutrients in the milk. In addition, there is ever more reason to believe that the important relationship between the mother and infant which develops during breastfeeding has a significant effect on the child's digestive capacities. Equally important is the role played by human milk in assuring immunisation to disease. Certain antibodies (IgG) are transmitted via the placenta which is permeable to them. This is not so with other antibodies (IgA and IgM). This means that babies are born without immunity to the diseases against which the latter provide protection. This includes those of gastro-enteric origin, which happen to be the leading causes of mortality among babies throughout the world. However, these antibodies IgA and IgM happen to be present in human milk in sufficient concentrations to provide protection against many gastro-enteric diseases such as those caused by E. Coli, and also against polio, though it appears that this immunisation only occurs if the corresponding antigens are present in the child's immediate environment.*

As Katz and Young[81] point out, it is likely that a real synergy exists between the nutritional, immunological, psycho-endocrinological and maternal responses, which foster infant development. It should be clear that as a result of millions of years of evolution breast-feeding has come to satisfy a large range of subtle requirements for both the infant, as part of the family system, and of the family as part of its ecosystem. It is indeed truly preposterous to suppose that it can be advantageously replaced by feeding an infant milk designed by evolution to satisfy a very different set of requirements — those of a baby ungulate — and contained in a bottle designed to provide but a crude imitation of its mother's teat.

Yet this is the sort of notion that is shaped on the basis of modern scientific method which is innocent of any theoretical concern with the structure and function of the natural systems which have co-evolved as the interrelated parts of the biosphere.

By concentrating on the parts, in fact, science *does not enable one to understand the nature of the whole.* Often it does not even enable one to realise *that there is a whole.* Thus until recently our scientists ignored the very notion of an ecosystem. If specific systems are part of a larger one, it means that they are subjected to a particular set of constraints which will enable them to act, for certain purposes at least, as a unit. Our failure

---

* Polio and Yellow Fever are, partly at least, diseases of hygiene. Children living in a natural environment in which they are exposed among other things to their own excreta, build up immunity against these diseases — so long, of course, as they are also fed on their mother's milk.

to recognise that we are part of a larger unit called an ecosystem implies that we are totally unaware of a whole set of constraints that must be observed if we are not to destroy that larger system. Even more astonishing is the fact that the very existence of a society as a natural system is still not generally understood by the scientific community. It is widely supposed that any group of heterogeneous people can constitute a society so long as they occupy the same area. This provides a rationale for today's pathological concern with the individual as opposed to the family and the community.

The notion that a society is a behavioural unit in its own right, a natural system in the sense that a biological organism is a natural system, is accepted only by a few thinking people who are familiar with the functioning of the tribal societies in which man has been organised during 99 per cent of his tenancy of this planet. Yet this notion is unquestionably correct, and our failure to accept it means that we ignore yet another set of extraordinarily important constraints to which human behaviour is, in normal conditions, subjected.

Thus the nature of the social problems such as crime, delinquency, alcoholism, drug addiction, etc., that our industrial society is suffering from, cannot conceivably be understood unless it is first understood that society is a natural system which normally provides its members with the requisite social environment. Only then can these ills be correctly interpreted as the pathological manifestations of social disintegration and, from the point of view of the victim, as the symptoms of social deprivation. Otherwise, these ills will continue to be interpreted as the signs of material deprivation — a convenient diagnosis in a society geared to the production of material goods, but one which, by promoting further industrialisation, and thereby further social disintegration, can only serve to aggravate the problems it is supposed to solve.

## Cause
Since all parts of a natural system are interrelated, it is also important to realise that a change in any one of them will inevitably affect the others directly and indirectly.* In fact each change is likely to give rise to a constellation of changes which will enable all the other parts affected to adjust to the new situation that the original change has given rise to. These

* This is true whatever be the sub-systems affected, i.e. whether it be an ecosystem, a population, a society, a family, an individual organism, a cell, or a molecule. They are all made up of subsystems in close interaction with each other. The complexity of the interaction between the different parts of an ecosystem was well illustrated by George Perkins Marsh. "The aquatic larvae of some insects," he wrote, "constitute, at certain seasons, a large part of the food of fresh water fish, while other larvae, in their turn, prey upon the spawn and even the young of their persecutors. The larvae of the mosquito and the gnat are the favourite food of the trout in the wooded regions where those insects abound. Earlier in the year the trout feeds on the larvae of

adjustments may be spread out over a period. The original effect is likely, in fact, to have a ripple effect that will be reflected in a large oscillation followed by increasingly smaller ones, as all the parts adapt to the original change, i.e. as the system becomes damped and thereby establishes a new position of equilibrium. Such a process clearly does not involve changes in one direction only. It is best regarded as a series of mutual adjustments and readjustments between the different parts of the system, each part affecting other parts and being in turn affected by them. Cause-and-effect relationships must thereby be regarded as involving not just two elements. They are, in fact, very much more subtle than empiricists seem to think they are. Each effect is likely to have a large number of different causes and because of their interaction it is likely to be only really explicable in terms of their combined actions, and also of the reactions to them.

What is more, if one wishes to explain the reason for each one of these changes, i.e. to determine what was its cause, one could do so in terms of a very large number of different models. The reason is of course that it occurred not to satisfy a single goal but all the varied requirements of the system. Unfortunately empiricists and scientists who accept the empiricists' notion of cause-and-effect are interested in one such explanation only: what is actually triggering off the change we are concerned with. On the basis of empiricist epistemology and of the reductionist method this is the only true cause, also the only one that can be studied in laboratory conditions.

We can illustrate this with reference to the elaborate life-cycle of the famous sitaris beetle as described by Bierens de Haan[83]: "Its larvae pass their development in the cells of the solitary bee anthophora", he writes, and "to this end the sitaris mother lays her eggs at the entrance of the nest of this bee. The young larvae hibernate in these galleries till, in spring, when the larvae are already seven months old, the young bees leave their nest. At that moment the sitaris larvae attach themselves to the hairy bodies of the bees. Now, these young bees are mostly males, as the males come out earlier than the females, and it is therefore necessary for the larvae to go over on to the females, which can only take place at the moment of copulation. If this succeeds, the larvae attach themselves to the thorax of the female bee and try to pass over to an egg of anthophora at

the Mayfly, which is itself very destructive to the spawn of the salmon, and hence, by a sort of house-that-Jack-built, the destruction of the mosquito, that feeds the trout, that preys on the Mayfly, that destroys the eggs that hatch the salmon, that pampers the epicure, may occasion a scarcity of this latter fish in waters where he would otherwise be abundant. Thus all nature is linked together by invisible bonds, and every organic creature, however low, however, feeble, however, dependent, is necessary to the well-being of some other among the myriad forms of life with which the Creator has peopled the earth."[82]

the moment this is laid. If this also succeeds, the larvae can feed first on the eggs and then on the contents of the cell of the anthophora.'' Only if it succeeds in accomplishing these series of feats can it hope to survive.

In the light of our knowledge of behaviour, we can provide the following 'causal' explanations for the laying of the egg by the sitaris beetle in front of the nest of the anthophora:-

1. We know that a response only occurs when there is an environmental demand for it. The situation which triggers off the requisite response is referred to as a stimulus. Thus, the sight of the nest acts as a stimulus releasing the egg-laying response. This is what is normally referred to by our scientists as a 'cause'.

2. If a system is capable of any response it is because it possesses the corresponding instructions (in this case, the egg-laying instructions) that have been built up phylogenetically and ontogenetically. These instructions too can be regarded as a 'cause'.

3. Neither the presence of the environmental stimulus nor the possession of the correct instructions are sufficient to explain a response. Behaviour, as we know, must be explained in terms of the interaction between a system and its environment. Thus the cause can be regarded as the sight of the nest as well as the possession of the egg-laying instructions.

4. We also know that a response must be regarded as but a step in a vast cumulative process. Thus we can regard the cause as being all of the previous steps in the phylogenetic and ontogenetic processes leading to this particular one.

5. We also know that processes forming part of the more general one must occur in the correct sequence. This must hold for the differentiated parts of the sitaris beetle's ontogenetic process. The necessary stimulus releasing the clinging response in the sitaris beetle is the sight of the male anthophora emerging from the nest. For this stimulus to be available, the female sitaris beetle must lay its egg in front of the anthophora's nest. This action can be taken as occurring *in order to permit the appearance of the stimulus which will trigger off the subsequent response.*

6. By the same token, we can say that it will occur to permit the subsequent response.

7. It is also known that no system can hope to survive unless its constituent parts are subjected to the constraints which will lead them to co-operate in ensuring its stability. This must be true of the sitaris beetle as a species. Thus one can say that the response will occur so as to favour the stability of the species.

These as well as a host of other such causal relationships, most of which are outside the scope of reductionist science, must be taken into account to provide a real explanation of the sitaris beetle's behaviour. It is simply ludicrous to insist that only one such relationship — the first one — can be regarded as a legitimate cause.

## Compartmentalisation

Another reason why science cannot replace a traditional cultural pattern is the established practice of dividing up knowledge into separate disciplines, each dealing with a set of things that appear to have something in common.

The biosphere, as I have constantly pointed out, is a single integrated system made up of closely integrated and hierarchically organised subsystems and sub-sub-systems. It is the product of a single integrated and hierarchically organised process. It has already been pointed out in 'The Religion of a Stable Society' that a traditional cultural pattern provides an integrated model of a society's relationship with its environment on the basis of which an integrated social behaviour pattern can alone be mediated. When primitive man considers any aspect of his environment he can thereby do so in terms of this complete model. It is unfortunately not the case among our scientific community of today, who can only see it in terms of their particular discipline. Quite clearly the biosphere cannot be understood in terms of a large number of separate and different disciplines.

Also, changes occurring within a specific field must inevitably cause changes in other fields about which a specialist would have very little knowledge. In addition, changes in other fields would also cause changes in his field which he would have no means of understanding. As a result, specialists are not only incapable of interpreting and predicting changes occurring outside their particular field of study but also, and this is possibly even worse, within it.

## Logistics

On logistical grounds alone, the whole scientific adventure is in any case a vain one. Even if it were possible to understand the functioning of a natural system by accumulating data concerning that of its parts, the amount of data required would be so astronomical that it would be logistically and financially impossible to obtain it. This fact has become evident in the specialised field dealing with the effect of pollution on natural systems, in which it has been found impossible to understand, on the basis of experiments carried out in laboratory conditions, the precise effect of introducing a new chemical substance into our environment. The reason is that man has already put something like two million pollutants into the environment and there are several thousand new ones every year. The World Health Organisation, according to Laird[84], receives between two and three thousand new ones each year for examination. WHO does not have any research facilities of its own so that these products must be farmed out to independent laboratories. For both financial and administrative reasons, less than ten per cent of them are examined in this way. Even then, these examinations are very superficial. They must be, for the problems involved in carrying them out satisfactorily are immense — and for all practical purposes, insuperable. One reason is that more often than not there is a synergic effect between different chemicals. For instance, the combination of Benzyspyrene with carbon dioxide can produce lung cancer in experimental animals.[85] Also animals infected with flu virus can contract lung cancer, if, at the same time, they have been exposed to artificial smog.[86]

DDT is regarded as presenting little hazard to marine life by virtue of the fact that it is only very slightly soluble in water. However it appears to be something like ten thousand times more soluble in oil, which means that the combination of DDT and oil can prove lethal to many forms of sea life.[87]

In addition, it is extremely difficult to examine the long-term effect of sub-lethal doses of different pollutants. Yet these are often as important if not more so than the more spectacular effects of large and sudden doses. For instance, a few parts per million of DDT in water can upset the temperature-regulating mechanism of young salmon.[88]

Sub-lethal amounts of DDT can be lethal when associated with falling temperature and starvation. This apparently explains why in a river in New Brunswick in 1969 there was considerable mortality among salmon during the cold weather than followed an earlier fish kill attributed to high levels of DDT.[88]

Minute doses of different pollutants can also have subtle effects on all sorts of behavioural mechanisms; on the ability of fish, for instance, to find their way about or to detect the presence of other fish.[88] Würster considers "that the subtle effects of CHS on avian reproduction have a greater overall impact on bird populations than an acute dose on more indirect mortality, even though a bird kill may seem more spectacular."[88]

Another problem is that of sampling. There is no guarantee that the levels measured during a given period are representative. Thus analyses of Rhine water have so far identified some 200 different pollutants and these are regarded as constituting perhaps no more than one-tenth of those present. Dr. Sonheimer, a chemist involved in this work, has said that there is no way of foreseeing "what will be floating in the river tomorrow . . . A cleaning process that works one day, works badly the next day."[89]

## Size of Samples Required

In view of this immense number of potentially harmful chemicals to which industrial man is exposed, and of their additive and possibly synergic effects, very small biological effects are significant, which, needless to say, render the problem even more difficult. As Epstein[90] writes, "assume that man is as sensitive to a particular carcinogen or teratogen as the rat or mouse. Assume further that this particular agent will produce cancer or a birth defect in one out of 10,000 humans exposed. Then the chances of detecting this in a group of 50 rats or mice, tested at ambient human exposure levels, are very low. Indeed, samples of 10,000 rats or mice would be required to yield one cancer or teratogenic event, over and above any spontaneous occurrences; for statistical significance perhaps 30,000 rodents would be needed."

Saffiotti[91] considers that to test potential carcinogens at very low levels, similar to those at which human populations may be exposed through residues in food, for instance, and in order to detect low incidences of tumours, about 10,000 mice would be required per experiment. Each experiment would cost about 15 million dollars, which means that to carry out a significant number of them would "block the nation's resources for long term bioassays for years to come and actually prevent the use of such resources for the detection of potent carcinogenic hazards from yet untested environmental chemicals."

Even then the results, for a number of reasons, would be highly contestable. To begin with such an approach assumes that there is a threshold dose at which a carcinogen is no longer effective. However, as Saffiotti maintains,[91] "there is presently no scientific basis for assuming that such a threshold would appear," a feeling that is shared by most authorities on environmental carcinogenesis today.

Secondly, these studies would in any case have to be confirmed by other tests carried out in different conditions, such as variations of diet, in the vehicles used, in the age of the animals, their sex etc. Each of these tests would then imply further megamouse experiments, what is more, they would clearly also have to be tested in combination with countless other chemicals, with which they may have additive or synergic effects.

The fact is that the problem cannot be solved in terms of what passes today for scientific method, and this is now accepted by a growing number of the scientists who have seriously considered all the factors involved.

Alvin Weinberg[92] is among them. He considers that a new 'trans-scientific' methodology is required for this purpose. On this subject it is worth quoting him in full.

"(The question) what is the effect on human health of very low levels of physical insult, can be stated in scientific terms; it can, so to speak, be asked of science, *yet it cannot be answered by science*. I have proposed the name trans-scientific for such questions . . .

"Let me use as an example of a trans-scientific question, the problem of low-level radiation dose . . . One may well ask, assuming the dose-response curve to be linear down to zero dose, how large an experiment would be required to demonstrate empirically that 170 millirems . . . would increase the mutation rate by the 0.5 predicted by the linear dose-response theory? The answer is that around 8 x 10 mice would be required to demonstrate a 0.5 per cent level at the 95 per cent confidence level. So large an experiment is beyond practical comprehension. The original question as stated is therefore, in my terminology, trans-scientific . . . Where low level effects are concerned, there will always be a trans-scientific residue."

How then would one solve such problems? The answer is by trying to establish what are the probable effects of radiation on biological organisms in terms of a non-disciplinary model of the relationship of biological organisms with their environment, i.e. by using the system's method. It is important to realise, however, that in this way one can only deal with probabilities. Formal proof or 'evidence' which many scientists crave for, cannot be obtained by this, or for that matter, any other method. When a situation is interpreted in terms of a model, the interpretation is simply a hypothesis. The brain like any other organisation of information or cybernism within the natural world can be regarded as a 'probability calculator' and it is on the basis of the models that they contain that adaptive responses in the natural world are mediated (Appendix IX).

In the case of radiation, it could be established, on the basis of a realistic model, that any increase over and above that which is obtained from natural sources, is likely to cause biological damage of some sort.

The question is, however, whether this systems method is really 'trans-scientific'? It all depends on how one defines the term 'science'. If science, by definition, must be compartmentalised into different watertight compartments, if it is to be concerned solely with the examination of the different parts of a system in isolation from each other, and with how things look rather than with what function they fulfil, then indeed the systems method is not 'scientific'. If on the other hand science is defined as the organisation of knowledge for the purposes of better understanding the world around us, then it must provide what can be regarded as the only true scientific method.

**Subjectivity**

But there is a further reason why objective science cannot replace subjective cultural patterns. It is that science is not objective. It is based on the empiricist thesis that knowledge can only be built up by observation, and observation, rather than be the objective process it is supposed to be, is in fact a *highly subjective one.* Let us see why this must be so. The perceptive process can be divided up functionally into three parts. The first is the detection of data, the second is their transduction into the informational medium used by the brain and the third is their interpretation, which is the critical part and also the one that seems to be least well understood by empiricists and by implication the scientists who have adopted the empiricist thesis.

## Detection

Let us consider detection. The first thing we must realise is that it is an active rather than a passive process. Data are indeed detected (just as a mine is detected by a mine detector) not just received, and detection is highly selective.[93] In fact, rather than accumulate data in a random fashion, as empiricists assume we do, we isolate the minute fraction that appears relevant to our behaviour pattern from that which does not. Thus, as Judson Herrick points out:

"The skin is sensitive to mechanical vibrations up to 1,552 per second, but beyond that point feels only a steady push. The ear is aware of sound travelling by wave lengths of 13 mm up to 12,280 mm, but does not hear sounds below or above these limits. The skin is aware of heat-waves only from .0008 mm to .1 mm long. The eye takes cognizance of light waves from .0008 mm to .0004 mm, but misses electric waves, ultra-violet waves, X-rays, gamma rays and cosmic rays, running from wavelengths of .0004 mm to .000,000,000,008 mm."[94]

This first genetically determined selection is complemented by a culturally determined one. At any given moment, we can detect but a minute fraction of those data which we are *genetically* equipped to detect — those that, in terms of our upbringing and experience within our particular culture, we have learned to regard as relevant to our behaviour, in the particular circumstances in which we find ourselves.

This also leads one to the essential consideration that detection can only occur *on the basis of a pre-existing model,* whose generalities reflect the experience of the species and whose particularities are largely based on the experience of the individual within his cultural group and in terms of which are calculated the relevance of different data to his behaviour pattern — yet another reason for rejecting the empiricist thesis. (See Appendix VII)

## The Subjectivity of Perception

The second step, that of the transduction of signals into the informational medium of the brain, appears straightforward though the exact mechanism involved has not, to my knowledge, been well established.

The third step in the process of perception, however, that of the interpretation of data, is even less objective than is detection, a fact that is alone sufficient to discredit the empiricist thesis as well as the scientific method that it underlies, both of which are based on the assumption of its objectivity.

Just as the relevance of data can only be determined by the light of an individual's mental model of his relationship with his environment, so it is only in the light of such a model that *they can be interpreted*.

Since the mental model must reflect an individual's personal experience within his cultural group, perception must be subjective. What a person actually sees will not only vary from person to person but will be influenced by all sorts of subjective factors, such as what he expects to see and what other people persuade him he should be seeing, etc. In fact perception, rather than provide objective information on the thing perceived, as Witkin[95] has so convincingly pointed out, tends to provide much more information on the personality of the perceiver (see Appendix X). A perception is therefore a hypothesis: that which appears to be the most probable in the light of an individual's phylogenetic and ontogenetic experience. (Appendix XII)

## The Subjectivity of Scientific Propositions

Contrary to what they themselves think, scientists proceed in precisely the same way. They select data on the basis of a preconceived model, in terms of which the data are subsequently interpreted.

This means that a scientific theory, rather than being reached 'inductively', in accordance with empiricist theory, must be regarded as postulated as that explanation of the available data that appears most probable on the basis of a specific model.

In this way, Le Verrier postulated, by purely mathematical means, the then unknown planet Neptune, as an explanation of certain otherwise inexplicable disturbances of the other planets. Later, as Reichenbach writes, ". . . when the German astronomer, Gelle, directed his telescope to the spot in the night sky that had been figured out by Le Verrier, he saw there a tiny speck that changed its position slightly from night to night, and the planet Neptune was discovered (1846)."[96]

Dirac postulated the positron as the most elegant way of explaining certain atomic phenomena inexplicable in terms of existing variables.

Epicurus and his disciple Lucretius postulated the atom, and Bohr the modern version of this ancient hypothesis. Watson and Crick proceeded in the same manner when developing the genetic code, as is revealed in Watson's book, *The Double Helix*.[97]

These discoveries are well-known. There is a tendency, however, to regard them as scientific curiosities — and as exceptions to the general rule that science develops inductively by the meticulous examination of impartially accumulated data in accordance with the empiricist thesis. I think, on the contrary, they are merely striking examples of what is the only possible method of science. If this were not the case, what would be the point of acquiring knowledge? In what way should a specialist be more capable of solving a problem pertaining to his speciality than the layman? There is indeed no reason to suppose that scientific explanations can take any other form.

Thus in the field of psychoanalysis, the existence of the unconscious, the theory of the Oedipus complex, the concept of repression, were simply postulates to explain certain aspects of pathological mental behaviour observed by Freud during his clinical practice, and the data that he collated served but to confirm their applicability, while that subsequently gathered by his antagonists served, in some cases, to invalidate them.

In the field of psychiatry, neuroses were postulated by Pavlov to explain the strange behaviour of the dogs that he frustrated experimentally. Schizophrenia, psychoses, manic depression, are all hypotheses postulated to explain related types of mental disorder. And so we can go on ad infinitum, and include in our list all the basic laws of science; the famous first and second laws of thermodynamics, Newton's gravity, Darwin's natural selection, Einstein's relativity. All are hypotheses postulated in like manner. Each offers that explanation which appears to fit in best with available information, all of which is collated directively according to its relevance in confirming or invalidating the hypothesis.

There is a hitch, however: an interpretation, whether of data detected during perception or of data collated by scientists during laboratory experiments, is only valid to the extent that the model adequately represents the relationship between the system and its environment. To be able to do so, the latter must be constantly changing in accordance with the changes occurring to the environment it represents.

In other words, if data are detected and their interpretation gives rise to a hypothesis whose adoption leads to unadaptive responses, then *the model itself must incur the appropriate modifications* so that the data can be interpreted in a way that *does* lead to adaptive responses.

In this way a system can monitor its responses, and any diversions from its optimum course can be corrected. If a model does not change in this way, and thereby ceases adequately to represent the environment, the interpretations of data based on it will be unsatisfactory and the responses based on such interpretations will be unadaptive. Cognitive maladjustment will have set in.

The trouble is that different parts of an organisation of information or cybernism in the natural world display *different degrees of inertia or nonplasticity* and cannot thereby be modified at will.

There is a very good reason for this. As we have seen, stable behaviour must be based on stable information. Stability is not immobility. An immobile system cannot be stable since it would not be adapting to a changing environment. If a system is to be stable, however, it is equally important that only the *particularities of its behaviour must change*, and hence only the particularities of the model on which this behaviour is based.

The generalities on the other hand must be *non-plastic except over a very long period*.

The reason is that the more general the information, the more important it is, since it colours all the other information in terms of which it is differentiated. Also, the more general it is, the longer the experience of the species or of the social group (in the case of cultural information) which it reflects, and the greater the certitude with which it can be predicted that the circumstances to which it mediates adaptive behaviour will be present.

Traditional man could predict *with confidence* that the circumstances that had been present for thousands of years were likely to continue being so. The whole cultural pattern of traditional societies therefore depended on the continued presence of these circumstances, and little or no provision was made for their possible absence. Thus, a fishing society living on the edge of a lake would assume that the lake did not go dry and that its fish population was not depleted. An Eskimo society living in the Arctic wastes would assume the continuance of the particular climatic conditions in which it lived. Neither the fishing society nor the Eskimo society would cater culturally for *drastic changes* in their basic relationship with their environment. Admittedly, if such changes occurred, then their cultural patterns would collapse, but in terms of their very long experience, there was no reason for them to suppose that they would conceivably do so.

It is important to note that an adaptive organisation of information or cybernism, in the natural world, will contain the optimum not the maximum amount of information. A system will not develop the capacity to detect signals and interpret them if *it does not have the capacity to adapt to the situations involved, or can only do so at the cost of disrupting its basic structure*. Yet to change the generalities of a pattern of information, and hence to seek to adapt to very radical changes, *must lead to* this disruption, which is precisely what the entire behaviour pattern has evolved to avoid.

Otherwise, it would provide the system with information that it could only adapt to by *destroying itself*. To avoid this contingency, *it must be adaptive for a system to interpret data that conflict with the generalities of its pattern of information in such a way so as to make them appear compatible with the generalities and thereby avoid the necessity of having to change them.* (See Appendix VIII.)

71

Interestingly enough, this is precisely what scientists do with information that conflicts with the basic generalities of the culture of industrialism with which nearly all of them have been imbued. The objective particularities of their 'scientific' world-view tend to be grafted on to its subjective generalities. Though this may be 'adaptive' to them as individuals, at least in the narrow sense of the term, in that it will contribute to their peace of mind, it is not adaptive to society as a whole, for it means that apparently objective 'evidence' will accumulate to rationalise the maintenance of our society on its present suicidal course towards ever further industrialisation.

The Procrustean interpretation of data can be adaptive, in fact, if it serves to preserve an adaptive cultural pattern. It is unadaptive, however, if its function is to preserve an aberrant and unadaptive cultural pattern.

There is no limit to the possible illustrations of this principle that one can provide. Consider one of Lord Zuckerman's 'scientific facts', taken from the speech at Stockholm,[77] already alluded to. He points to the "increasing physical and intellectual violence to which we are all subjected" and attributes this to the frustration of not being able to increase our standard of living quickly enough. This is clearly not a 'scientific fact', but simply one of a large number of possible interpretations of the available data. What is more it is probably not that which is best reconcilable with available knowledge, but rather that which best suits his desire to prove that the *Limits to Growth* argument is wrong and that economic growth is necessary.

It may be argued that this problem is overcome when one is dealing with precisely quantified data. However, the results of even the most precise measurements often tend to be rationalised so as not to conflict with cherished subjective beliefs (Appendix XI). Defenders of industrialisation still maintain, for instance, that the cancer rate is not increasing in industrial society. What has increased, they maintain, is our ability to diagnose it. This myth is only being exploded as we are beginning to know more about the health of tribal societies among whose members the incidence of cancer happens to be negligible.

In the same way Lord Zuckerman refuses to admit that lead pollution is worsening in spite of the fact that lead levels in the air we breathe and the water we drink are everywhere on the rise. "The risk of being poisoned today" he writes, "is probably as small as at any time since lead started to be mined. *But we have now developed the ability to detect the presence of this element.*"

The fact is that measurements, even when extremely precise, constitute data and *science does not provide a precise methodology for interpreting them. As a result they will amost certainly tend to be inter-*

72

*preted in that way which best satisfies the basic generalities of a scientist's cultural pattern. For this reason science, when it concerns itself with matters in which man has a psychological stake, is barely less subjective than is the culture of a traditional society. To substitute one for the other is but to substitute the culture of industrialism for the cultural pattern of a traditional society, and hence to divert a society from the goal of stability to that of ever increasing instability and eventual collapse.*

## Objective Knowledge

Objective knowledge, in fact, plays no part in the evolutionary process of which man is but after all the product. The information used by natural systems at all levels of organisation is not objective but subjective. Genetic information, for instance, is not objective. It is specific to a particular individual as a member of a particular species. Cultural information is not objective. It is specific to a particular individual as a member of a particular cultural group. In fact, one can go further and say that, as the biosphere has evolved out of the primeval dust, and as complexity and variety have built up, so has there been a corresponding build-up of the subjective information associated with this evolutionary development. *In fact, informational complexity and variety are essential for achieving systemic complexity and variety.* This means that to substitute a single organisation of objective information for the multitudinous organisations of subjective information, which are used to control the behaviour of natural systems, *is to reverse evolutionary trends and hence to foster informational entropy.*

It could be argued that objective information also displays order or negative-entropy. This is true only in the sense that the technosphere displays order. Order is but another word for organisation. Things are organised for a particular purpose, i.e. to satisfy a particular goal. Random organisation is a contradiction in terms. Now the goal of the technosphere is very different from that of the biosphere. The former is designed to provide man, one of the myriad forms of life which inhabit this planet, with the maximum of comfort and convenience, whereas the latter, being concerned with the maintenance of its overall stability, is designed to cater for the requirements of all, not just one of the forms of life which inhabit it, to the extent that they contribute towards its proper functioning. These two organisations of matter, moreover, are in competition with each other, since the technosphere can only maintain itself by extracting resources from the biosphere and consigning to it its waste products. Hence, from the point of view of the biosphere, *the technosphere constitutes waste or randomness or, in fact, entropy.* Similarly, from the point of view of that organisation of subjective information associated with the biosphere, *objective information constitutes entropy.*

73

*It has played no role in building up the biosphere; and it is thereby only vis-à-vis the technosphere that objective information displays negative-entropy.*

### Informational Entropy and Centralisation
The destruction of informational variety, i.e. of informational organisation within the biosphere, is essential if information is to be centralised so that a single body of scientific knowledge replaces a large number of traditional cultures as a basis for social control.

Consider the island of New Guinea, where there are at present seven hundred different tribal groups, each with its own religio-culture. If the country were modernised, these religio-cultures would inevitably be destroyed; the population would be herded into large industrial complexes and the children would soon be subjected to the standard Western type of education.

These religio-cultures have developed over the course of thousands of years, not at random, but for a specific purpose — that of enabling the tribal groups in question to achieve a stable relationship with their environment. This they achieve remarkably well, as can be attested by all those who have examined the behaviour of tribal societies. However, it is considered by us that their behaviour would be more adaptive were it based on a single organisation of information — that which objectively reflects the world they, as well as countless other social groups throughout the world, happen to live in.

We forget, however that a society is a natural system, and that *its culture is an integral part of it*, that part which ensures its control. If one is willing to remove an integral part of a society's control system in this way, why not do the same with its other constituent parts? Why not, for instance, centralise genetic information? Why not start a world genetic data bank, so that animals wishing to reproduce themselves in a modern and 'scientific' way, whether they be fiddler-crabs, dung-beetles, or humans need but contact the data bank to obtain, by the aid of some giant computer, all the genetic information that they may require for this purpose? However ridiculous this suggestion may sound, in behavioural terms, the same principle is involved. In both cases it means counteracting the processes leading to the evolutionary development of normal control mechanisms. Such action is anti-evolutionary and can only lead to an increase in randomness.

Let us push the argument still further. If, in the interests of centralisation, we deprive the inhabitants of New Guinea of their social control mechanisms, why do we not do the same for the other mechanisms involved in their life processes? Why do we not set up, for their benefit, a single computerised liver for instance, or a complete digestive system

74

which would deal with all the digestive processes of the island's population, thereby freeing it of digestive worries and letting it concentrate on more progressive activities such as watching TV or going to football matches? Once more the example may appear absurd. But in cybernetic terms it is not absurd at all. Natural systems must be self-regulating if they are to be stable. *A control-mechanism is an integral part of a system. Remove it and the system disintegrates, just as would an organism if one were to remove its liver or its digestive system. That is why traditional societies have not survived the destruction of their cultures.*

### Differentiation

Another basic reason why the centralisation of information must be counter-productive is that it prevents its proper differentiation. It is important to realise that the original instructions mediating any behavioural process in the natural world are of a very general nature. These instructions are then differentiated at each level during their implementation so as to adapt them as precisely as possible to environmental requirements at each level.

It is well known that the information, for instance, contained in a fertilised egg is not enough to give rise to the foetus. It only contains the general information, and considerably more information is built up during the development of the embryo. It is also clear that an adult is not simply the product of the information contained in the foetus, but is the product of a very long process during which basic instructions are differentiated to satisfy the particular exigencies of the life style that it adopts as it grows up. The principle is well illustrated by the behaviour of an army.

It is not even remotely conceivable for a General to issue a complete and detailed Plan of Action which will be observed to the letter at every echelon down to that of the individual soldier. It would be logistically impossible for him to monitor all the details of a military campaign; the map in his operations room would have to be massive and the number of people required to keep it up to date and transmit the necessary instructions would probably be considerably greater than the number of soldiers actually in the field. Besides, the time lag between the reception of a signal from the lowest echelon of command and the transmission of the appropriate instructions would be too long.

Consider, for instance, a soldier who is about to be shot by an enemy sniper hidden behind a tree. If he had to send a message to the General at Headquarters, ten miles away, to obtain permission to pull the trigger and shoot the sniper, his chances of survival would be very slim indeed. Yet this is precisely what would be involved were all information to be centralised.

The fact is that a general can only deal wth important matters, i.e.

signals that threaten his army as a whole rather than a small section of it, and the instructions he gives to deal with the corresponding threat must be differentiated at each echelon of command so as to adapt them to local requirements. There is no example in nature of any behavioural process that functions in any other way. The inefficiency involved would be immense, the logistical problems insuperable. It is not generally realised that this is what is involved in substituting scientific knowledge for that contained in traditional cultural patterns.

The centralisation of information has a further consequence, that of rendering ineffective the control mechanisms of all the intermediary social groupings which must thereby tend to disintegrate. Society is thereby deprived of the intermediary self-regulating groupings that provides it with its hierarchical structure and enables it to function as a self-regulating natural system.

It is not surprising that self-regulating social systems will, as we have seen, reject information that does not fit in with the model or world view they have developed as part of their cultural pattern. This is clearly adaptive in order to maintain the integrity of their culture and of the behavioural pattern associated with it. When a culture breaks down, however, the society involved becomes open to information from the outside. With the spread of Western ideas among the educated 'elites' of the countries of the Third World, industrial practices that may be acceptable in the short term, at least in the West, are indiscriminately applied in other parts of the world where conditions are very different and in which their application can only lead to disastrous results.

Modern agriculture, for instance, has been devised largely on the basis of the experience of European countries enjoying a temperate climate. Its indiscriminate application to tropical areas were climatic and soil conditions are quite different has led to wholesale soil destruction and desertification.

Our ideas of government are just as sociocentric, and their export to Africa and Asia has led to the erosion of traditional cultures and to the setting up in their place of unstable political regimes that are little more than parodies of their already largely unsuccessful European counterparts.

Thus, the transmission of information in a hierarchically organised natural system, occurs in an orderly manner, so as to assure orderly behaviour at each level and hence of that of the system as a whole. Once information becomes highly centralised, however, there is no longer any mechanism for assuring its orderly transmission, and the behaviour it mediates becomes random and increasingly unstable.

**The Systems Method**
I have attempted up to now to show that reductionist science based on

empiricist philosophy cannot serve as a basis for social control. But must science be reductionist? Also, must it be based on empiricism? Can one not develop a science in terms of which one can understand the world around us, and on the basis of which an adaptive social behaviour pattern can be mediated? Clearly if there is such a science, then it must be that which currently goes under the name of General Systems.

Let us look a little more closely into how it works and what it consists of to see whether it does in fact overcome the problems of present day scientific method.

The systems method consists of three basic operations.

The first is referred to as 'systems analysis'. It consists in determining what are the variables that must be taken into account in order to understand a given situation. Variables are not selected because they happen to fall within the scope of a particular discipline, for the systems method is non-disciplinary. Nor are the variables chosen, as we shall see, simply from among those that happen to be observable, because the systems method is not based on empiricism. They are chosen, as in the case of normal detection, because a change in their value will affect that of the other variables that are used in the model. The fact that the variables used do not simply correspond to sensations as do those used by empiricists has very important implications. Empiricists are principally concerned with describing in minute detail all the subtle ways in which natural systems differ from each other. Real science, however, begins when we reach the next stage, that of determining what natural systems have in common, for it is only then that data are being organised to constitute a model. Empiricists are incapable of doing this, since it would mean including in the same category things that fall within the scope of many different disciplines and also things that *appear very different* and whose similarity for specific purposes empiricists would thereby refuse to admit.

For instance, if one compared the behaviour of a human with that of a simpler form of life, such as, say a honeypot ant, empiricists would almost certainly look up in horror and say, "You cannot compare an intelligent being, capable of conscious cultural behaviour and possessing a conscience and free will, with a vile, brutish thing like a honeypot ant, whose behaviour can be explained entirely in terms of the workings of blind instinct." From this it is implied that, because *they look different*, they should be classified for all purposes in *different scientific categories*, and, further, that it is illegitimate to make comparisons between such dissimilar categories.

For certain purposes, however, they happen to be very similar. For instance, they both obey the laws of physics, chemistry, and biology. They both have eyes and other sensing mechanisms, are capable of respiration, digestion, excretion, locomotion, communication and

77

reproduction. *In fact, the generalities of their behaviour pattern are so similar that they can be described in terms of the same basic variables. It is only in the particularities that they display any appreciable behavioural divergencies.*

To oppose the formulation of general principles concerning the behaviour of such seemingly different forms of life on empirical grounds, i.e. because of their apparently divergent behavioural particularities, is, as von Bertalanffy writes, ". . . the same as if one would criticise Newton's law because it draws a loose 'analogy' between apples, planets, ebb and tide, and many other entities; or if one would declare the theory of probability meaningless because it is concerned with the 'analogy' of games of dice, mortality statistics, molecules in gas, the distribution of hereditary characteristics, and a host of other phenomena." [98] In fact, it is totally unjustified.

The next phase in the systems method is referred to as 'modelling'. This consists in determining just how the variables selected are related to each other. What is more, the relationships taken into account, if the model is to be effective in mediating adaptive responses, cannot just be one-way cause-and-effect relationships.

If the model is properly constructed, it will take into account all sorts of other relationships, as mentioned earlier in this chapter.

In this way yet another deficiency of present day scientific method can be overcome. Once this has been achieved an effective method is available, capable of representing the relationship of a system with its environment *for the purposes of controlling at least certain types of responses.*

The third stage is referred to as 'simulation'. It is functionally the same as perception. In both cases data are interpreted in the light of the model, and the more elaborate the model, the greater the amount of *relevant* data, and the extent to which they are interconnected or organised, i.e. the more one knows about the subject involved, the more critical is the interpretation likely to be.

It is only by building up an elaborate scientific model by means of the systems method that one can reduce to the minimum our built-in tendency towards subjectivity, largely because it forces us to face *all the assumptions and implications of a particular hypothesis in the light of the best organisation of information* that is available on the subject.

## The Limitations of the Systems Method

The systems method, however, has many limitations. At the moment, for instance, people who apply it are as infatuated with quantification as our normal reductionist scientists. The whole subject of general systems is becoming increasingly technical. Measuring is replacing thinking just as it is in other fields. In this way systems scientists, like reductionist scientists, still tend to be using quantifiable variables to the exclusion of the very *many important ones which have not been quantified*, and it is difficult to tell to what extent it is possible to get round this problem.

Let us look very briefly at the question of quantifying variables. It is generally assumed that by doing so they are rendered more precise. This is not so. A quantifiable variable tends to be of value because it is held to be an inidcator of a particular state of a system, natural or man-made. Thus, the measurement of an individual's body temperature is taken to provide information on his state of health. This may well be so, but it must be admitted that this input is of a very rough and ready kind. It provides, in fact, but a rule of thumb that has the advantage of convenience and little more. In the same way, the GNP and the Balance of Payments are quantifiable variables in terms of which it is customary to judge the health of the economy. They, too, are extremely crude and their value also resides in their convenience. To measure the health of a river in terms of its oxygen content, as tends to be done today, is also very simplistic, as it is to measure the fertility of the soil in a particular area in terms of the short-term yields of the crops that can be grown there. The use of these quantifiable variables to represent more complex situations that are otherwise difficult to quantify is only justified on the basis of a specific world-view. In terms of an ecological world-view, only the first of the rules of thumb can be accepted. On the other hand, alternative rules of thumb could be proposed for quantifying such situations.

Durkheim [99] suggested that the suicide rate be taken to provide a rule of thumb for measuring social deprivation and hence social disintegration. However, this may be useful in some societies and not in others. People from different societies are likely to react in different ways to the disintegration of their social environment. Opler, for instance, has shown that Italians tend to react to such a situation by becoming schizophrenics, while the Irish seek refuge in alcoholism. In other words, a quantifiable criterion which may be suitable in one case is not in another.[100]

The important thing to realise is that quantification does not lead to precision.

The main advantage of quantification, however, seems to lie in the fact that *rules exist for establishing precise relationships between different numbers*, even though these relationships may not coincide with any great precision with those that actually obtain between the processes in the real world that these numbers represent. Nevertheless quantification does allow one to build a model that can be *seen* to function so that the effect of a change in the value of any one variable on all the other variables used in the model can be much more easily appreciated.

Another problem is that the systems method requires multi-disciplinary cooperation which is extremely difficult to come by. Specialists in the different disciplines have developed different terminologies and methodologies, and real contact between them is almost impossible save on a very superficial basis. This situation is getting worse rather than better. Prestige is acquired by becoming more technical and more esoteric rather than less so. What we are in fact witnessing is the operation of a basic psychological tendency that leads to territoriality. Non-specialists must be kept out of one's territory at any cost, while ambitious men will often carve out their own academic territory on the slightest pretext. Look at cybernetics — the creation of Norbert Wiener. Here at last was a tool which could be used for unifying the sciences. It was not to be. Not only has it become increasingly technical, but its domain has already been sliced up by ambitious academics. Von Bertalanffy called his territory General Systems, while Forrester has chosen Systems Dynamics as his domain, and I am sure there will be many more. In this way, instead of merging the various disciplines, it has actually given rise to at least two new ones.

If we can predict the failure of multi-disciplinary research with total confidence, however, it is because the different disciplines, having evolved independently, *are not compatible with each other*.

Modern medicine, as Boyden points out, is irreconcilable with evolutionary theory.[15] Modern dentistry with its dependence on X-rays, cannot be reconciled with radiobiology; modern economics is incompatible with both anthropology, as Polanyi has shown,[64] and ecology as Boulding, in particular, has demonstrated.[101] It is also incompatible, as Georgescu Roegen[102] has pointed out, with the laws of thermodynamics.

For effective multi-disciplinary work to take place, specialists would have to admit that many of the principles on which their disciplines are based are simply not true. Can we expect them to do so? Can we really expect people who have established a reputation in a particular field after years of hard work to admit that their work is based on faulty assumptions? Of course not. They can be counted upon to rationalise any extraneous information which appears to menace their professional status in such a way that it will cease to do so. The effect of this natural psychological tendency, however, is to render multi-disciplinary research largely impracticable.

Let us assume, rightly or wrongly, that we can overcome these problems and that the systems method becomes generally accepted throughout the academic world. Would we now be in a position to guide our society along its present course towards ever increasing industrialisation in such a way as to avoid the problems we are now encountering in an ever more acute form? The answer is undoubtedly in the negative. The sheer mass of data required to monitor the effect of developmental activities on the environment make the task impossible. As we are coming to realise, very minute changes can have a serious effect on the behaviour of natural systems. We have seen how this is so in the case of pollution. As Reid Bryson points out[103] very small climatic changes have shifted rainfall patterns causing whole cultures to disappear. As Letitia Obeng[104] has also noted, an increase of temperature of only 2 per cent above average in tropical waters could totally disrupt a marine ecosystem whereas a 3 per cent change could eradicate most of the important fish in the tropics.

To take into account the enormous number of factors that could, by themselves or in different combinations, lead to small changes of this sort is simply not possible. A model capable of taking into account the numerous factors that could, by themselves or in different combinations, lead to small changes of this sort, could never be built. These factors, or combinations of factors, would have to be looked at in the wider context of the whole situation represented by the model and logistically this would be a greater problem than looking at them separately as is done by reductionist science. For instance, simply to take into account all those that could be involved in the determination of weather changes goes, according to Flohn[105], "much beyond the capacity of our computer to handle completely."

To effectively monitor global developments we would probably need a model that was little short of a to-scale replica of the process it presented, i.e. of man and his interrelationship with the biosphere.

**Environmental Modification**
The real value of the systems method is to enable one to understand basic principles which tend to be ignored by reductionist science with its pre-occupation with details. A model taking into account such principles would serve above all to show how unadaptive was the course on which our industrial society is set.

Let us look a little more closely into the adaptive process. In the bio-sphere, a system can adapt, either by modifying its environment to satisfy its own requirements, or by itself undergoing change to satisfy such requirements in a changed environment. In practice, both strategies are resorted to. We have seen that the justification for science must be to permit rapid and radical adaptation over and above that which a traditional culture would permit. When rapid and radical change is required, however, the former strategy is the only possible one. It is quicker and easier to adapt man to living in a cold climate, for instance, by building him houses with central heating, double glazing, etc. than by bringing about those physical changes in him which would enable him to support the cold weather. Thus in practice, objective information simply *permits environmental change*. If this environmental change were not

81

regarded as desirable there would be no reason for replacing traditional subjective information with apparently objective information.

## Consequences of Changing the Environment

However, there is a limit to the extent to which a system can modify its environment before it ceases to become adaptive to it. Let us not forget that behaviour is directive and tends towards increasing stability. This is precisely what the evolutionary process has done. It has adapted us to our environment in such a way that the discontinuities to which we are likely to be subjected are reduced to a minimum. When we modify this environment, however, beyond a certain point, it begins to divert from that to which we have been adapted by our evolution. Such environmental modification is thereby *anti-evolutionary*. It must increase instability and hence the discontinuities to which we are subjected.

Indeed as we diverge from the environment to which we have been adapted, both biologically by means of phylogeny and ontogeny, and socially by means of our society's cultural evolution and of our own education, so are we *creating a host of maladjustments at different levels of organisation.*

Thus, it is becoming increasingly apparent that we are subject to a whole new range of diseases which are unknown in tribal societies living in their natural habitat. I refer to cancer, in particular cancer of the lungs and bowel, ischaemic heart disease, diabetes, diverticulitis, and tooth-decay. These are already becoming known as the 'diseases of civilisation'.[106] Boyden refers to them as the 'diseases of biological maladjustment'.[15] They appear to be caused by environmental factors which were absent in primitive conditions and the further we diverge from such conditions, as measured by per capita GNP, the *greater is their incidence.*

It is also becoming increasingly clear that we are faced with an ever wider range of social disorders, which were absent in 'primitive' conditions. Their incidence also appears to increase with per capita GNP — I refer, of course, to crime, delinquency, alcoholism, illegitimacy, suicide, etc. These are best regarded as the symptoms of 'social maladjustment'.

The notion, of course, that man is only capable of adapting to that range of environmental changes which can be catered for by a traditional cultural pattern conflicts with the notion that the substitution of a framework of objective knowledge for his traditional cultural knowledge increases his range of adaptations.

It is generally considered, however, that these problems are of no consequence, for, as a result of man's infinite ingenuity, and of the omnipotence of science and technology, he will easily be able to overcome them. If it is possible to maintain this myth, it is largely because the concept of adaptability has never been adequately defined. If we define it, as we should, in terms of the capacity of a system to maintain its stability, then to say that man is infinitely adaptable is simply not true. Man, by means of science and technology, is capable of counteracting discontinuities, *but only very superficially and at great cost in terms of reduced stability,* and hence with the prospect of greater discontinuities in the future which science and technology will eventually be unable to deal with.

The reason is that technological remedies do little more than mask the symptoms of a disease, thereby rendering it more tolerable and serving in this way to perpetuate it. Their effect is *to accommodate trends rather than to reverse them,* and hence to permit yet further deviations from the optimum environment to which we have been adapted by our evolution, and to give rise thereby to further maladjustments at all levels. This is precisely what happens, for instance, when we combat tooth decay by engaging more dentists and providing people with false teeth. The real solution to the problem of tooth decay is to make sure people eat a better diet so that their teeth do not decay. This, however, is difficult to achieve without reducing the importance of the food processing industry and modifying life styles so that people produce most of their own food, all of which we are not prepared to do.

In the same way, we fight the growing crime wave by manufacturing more burglar alarms and armoured cars, and by engaging more policemen, whereas the real solution is to recreate a sound society in which crime does not occur. This, however, would mean transforming society so that it resembled that in which man lived for the first few million years of his tenancy of this planet, and hence largely reversing most of the trends that we have been taught to identify with progress, a policy that is, at least at the present time, totally unacceptable.

### Cognitive Maladjustment
Changing the environment too radically must also give rise to another form of maladjustment whose implications have too rarely been faced. We have seen that perception cannot serve as the basis for objective knowledge, but this should be of no concern since, as we have also seen, objective knowledge plays no part in the strategy of nature. What is essential, however, is that perception should provide us with the *appropriate* subjective knowledge, that *which will lead to adaptive behaviour on our part.*

This, our perceptive apparatus, succeeds in doing admirably, just as it does in the case of all other forms of life, so long *as we remain in the environment to which we have been adapted phylogenetically and ontogenetically*. As our environment diverges from this, however, so are our perceptions ever less useful in understanding it and in helping us to adapt to it. It becomes, to use Forrester's [17] expression, increasingly 'counter-intuitive' not, however, because it is too complex, as he supposes, *but because we have no evolutionary experience of it.*

Thus, whereas our Paleolithic ancestors had no difficulty in understanding what was their relationship with the cave bear and the woolly mammoth, we have no means of understanding what are the implications of subjecting our children to X-rays, or permitting a nuclear power station to be built in the vicinity of our homes, of allowing supersonic transport to erode the ozone belt which shields our planet from solar radiation, of cutting down the world's remaining stands of tropical forest, or of countenancing, in fact, the industrialisation process itself.

Ross Hume Hall [107] points out how we are cognitively maladjusted to modern processed foods and how, as a result we are incapable of behaving adaptively towards them, "Nature endowed us with the capacity to determine nutritional quality and safety of food so long as it was natural," he writes. "For example, we can distinguish between corn fresh from the stalk and corn a day old. Colour, smell and texture are all sensations we use in assessing the nutritive value of food. But all this changes in the modern era of fabricated food. Bakery products and candy appear yellow because they have been treated with a coal tar derivative. Bread, soups and pickles seem tastier because they contain sugar. Meat appears fresher because it contains sodium nitrites to inhibit bacterial growth.

"Net result: *the taste of fabricated food is no reliable guide to freshness, nutritional quality, or whether the food will eventually kill you.* The responsibility for safety and nutritional quality of what we eat has passed into the hands of scientists and administrators who, within the jurisdictional confines of the FDA and other regulatory bodies, provide a corporate surrogate for ensuring the healthfulness of your food."

In other words, as the environment diverges from the norm and perception ceases to provide a basis for adaptive responses, our self-regulatory mechanisms break down and we must now be governed 'asystemically' by some external agent. This violates the basic principle of cybernetics, which is that stability can only be achieved by self-regulation.

We can now begin to explain why objective information, even when properly organised to constitute a non disciplinary model of our relationship with our environment, can play no role in the strategy of nature. *It can only serve to bring about environmental changes to which we are incapable of adapting.*

The subjective information contained in traditional cultural patterns undoubtedly gave rise to far more adaptive responses. This can be demonstrated empirically. Indeed modern agriculture, based as it is on the scientific information that has led to the development of artificial pesticides and agricultural machinery, is highly unsatisfactory from the biological, social and ecological point of view. Traditional agriculture was very much more satisfactory on all these counts.[108] The same can be said of our efforts to impose scientifically determined diets on the people of the Third World who have come within the orbit of our industrial society. Wherever this has happened, as Hughes and Hunter[109] and other nutritionalists have pointed out, nutrition and health have invariably suffered.

Modern methods of population control, depending as they do on the distribution of birth control devices, has also been a failure. The problem is a social not a technological one. People must be motivated to have less children and this has only been achieved when controls have been built into the cultural pattern of traditional societies.

Modern medicine, based as it is on scientific knowledge derived from millions of hours of scientific research, is proving equally unsatisfactory. That its apparent triumphs have been short lived is rapidly being revealed by the reappearance of many of the infectious diseases it is supposed to have eliminated and also by its impotence to deal with the so-called diseases of civilisation whose incidence continues inexorably to increase among the inhabitants of the industrial world. It is no coincidence, in fact, that, everywhere, there is now a renewed interest in the medicine of traditional societies which, in the long run, far better satisfies basic biological, social and ecological exigencies.

The mass educational system we have set up, so as to imbue our children with scientific and technological knowledge, is proving equally unsuccessful — if the goallessness and alienation of our youth is to be taken as a criterion. Indeed, to prevent total social breakdown, it is urgent that 'education' be seen again in its true light as but another word for socialisation, i.e. as a means of communicating to our youth that cultural information which will enable them to fulfil their functions as members of their families and communities.

In fact, if one were to attempt to determine, in terms of a general model, what would be the ideal behaviour pattern of a traditional society living in its natural environment, the answer would undoubtedly be: that which it already displayed, *that in fact, which had come into being as a result of its cultural evolution and which must enable it to fulfil its ecological* functions within the biosphere like any of the other natural systems that comprise it.

In other words, the greatest contribution that science can make is to demonstrate that *there is no need for it.*

# Our Fatal Illusions

It is basic to the culture of Western man that, rather than being part of Nature, he is above it. This leads to the preposterous notion that his behaviour cannot be subjected to the sort of analysis used to understand the behaviour of other forms of life. Whereas atoms, molecules, cells, even complex multicellular but non-human animals can be described in the comparatively precise terms of physics, chemistry, biology, and cybernetics, it is widely believed that human beings and the societies in which they are organised can only be described in terms of a much vaguer language, that of the humanities, and that the precise prediction of their behaviour is not even remotely conceivable. We justify this thesis by establishing all sorts of totally artificial barriers between man and other forms of life.

## Consciousness

One such barrier is consciousness. But can it really be regarded as a frontier separating the mental activities of man from those of lower forms of life? A little reflection will make it apparent that this term is a purely subjective one, and cannot, thereby, serve as a unit of an objective scientific model.

As Rapoport[110] writes: "When the vitalist says that certain living organisms are characterised by 'consciousness', and that this property necessitates a postulate of a special principle, he has not really identified the 'peculiar events'. No matter how direct is our awareness of our own 'consciousness', this term has no objectively identifiable referent."

It is conceivable of course that the subjective notion of 'consciousness' could be associated with a precise teleonomic variable of a scientific model. In this way, it would be possible to determine what there was really in common between mental processes that appeared to us as conscious, and in what way these differed from others that appeared to us unconscious.

I think that this is in fact possible. Thus a signal interpretable as denoting the presence of a book that I was not looking for and that was situated in its normal place in my library would display both low relevance to the situation and low improbability. As a result, I would probably not be conscious of its presence when looking in its direction.

On the other hand, a signal denoting the presence of a book that I was looking for, though situated in its normal place in my library, would have high relevance and low improbability and, when looking in its direction, I would be conscious of seeing it.

A signal denoting the presence of a book that I was not looking for, but which occupied an unexpected position in my library, would display low relevance but high improbability. It would therefore be probable that, if I looked in its direction, I would be conscious of seeing it. On the other hand I would unquestionably be conscious of seeing a book that I was not only looking for, but that, at the same time, occupied an unexpected position in my library, as the signal that could be interpreted as denoting its presence would have both high relevance and high improbability.

If we accept that consciousness is needed for interpreting a signal displaying high information value vis-à-vis the receiving cybernism, then to say that humans alone display consciousness must be false, since, whereas it is certainly true that humans are capable of interpreting signals having a higher information value than can other animals, the difference is but one of degree.

## Vitalism

The physical world as depicted by nineteenth century science was grim and deterministic. Man had a psychological stake in carefully delimiting that area which was science's domain, so as to preserve that of human behaviour from its incursions, and to maintain thereby the illusion of the freedom of the will. For this purpose, a mysterious force was postulated that Bergson called the 'elan vital', a resuscitation of Aristotle's 'entelechy', a notion usually referred to today as 'vitalism', whose presence is supposed to distinguish mind from matter. Thus, if living things appeared to behave in a goal-seeking or directive manner, it was because they were 'willed to do so' by this mysterious force.

There are many objections to such a thesis. First of all, the twentieth century notion of matter no longer corresponds to that which prevailed previously. Among other things, *it is no longer deterministic*, since Heisenberg[11] showed that the behaviour of atoms, like that of humans, could not be predicted with certainty. Thus it is not from this quarter that the notion of the freedom of the will has most to fear. Secondly, it has been established over and over again that *there is in fact no frontier between the animate and the inanimate*. Organic substances usually associated with living things are constantly being synthesised from inorganic ones, and natural systems such as viruses have characteristics both of living and of non-living things at different stages during their life-cycles. Thirdly, the vitalist thesis conveys very little information. The mysterious force postulated to differentiate men from other animals is so mysterious that it cannot be explained in terms of the variables of any vaguely scientific model of behaviour. As Rapoport[110] writes:

"The objection of the anti-vitalist against the vitalist's notion of 'life-force' or the like is not so much on the grounds that this supposed principle does not fit in with the known laws governing the behaviour of matter (it would be foolhardy to assume that we know all such laws); but on the ground that the proposed 'life force' is not a 'principle'. *It explains nothing. It is only a name for a supposed principle and will remain a name until the vitalist says more about how this life force is supposed to operate.*"

## The Freedom of the Will

Among the many attributes of man that are supposed to distinguish him from less privileged animals is the possession of a 'free will'. This concept has important theological and legal implications, since, if the will is not 'free', then man is not capable, by his own efforts, of modifying his lot. The latter must be predetermined by some mysterious force, thereby freeing him from any responsibility for his sins or crimes.

What does this freedom of the will imply? To answer this, let us first see what is meant by 'free' and 'will'. The 'will' is meant to be the mechanism issuing those instructions in terms of which our behaviour pattern can be explained. We have seen, however, that the latter is mediated by a hierarchical organisation of behavioural centres. Is the will then just another word for this organisation? I doubt it, since such an organisation can be found determining the behaviour of natural systems at all levels of complexity. It is present in dogs, frogs, amoebas, microbes, viruses, and undoubtedly even in atoms. What, then, is the will? I think it will be found that it is normally associated with conscious behaviour. Man, it is thought, is conscious of what he does and must therefore be capable of choice. We have seen that only those instructions mediated by the centres in the upper strata of cybernismic organisation can be regarded as 'conscious'. Psychoanalysis, hypnosis and motivation research reveal only too plainly that nearly all our behaviour is mediated unconsciously. It is probably more precise to say that *we are in fact conscious of the particularities*

88

*of decisions whose generalities are determined unconsciously.*

If the 'will' is taken to be the 'conscious' part of the organisation of behavioural centres, it can be shown that it is responsible for the most trivial and superficial instructions, and not for the general or important ones. This does not correspond to one's notion of the will.

Let us now turn our attention to the use of the word 'free'. In what sense can either a behaviour pattern, or part of one, be 'free'? We have seen that one of the essential features of order is limitation of choice. If this does not obtain, behaviour is random, disorderly, and unpredictable. Limitation of choice is ensured accumulatively. At each stage of development, a system acquires new instructions, which will further limit the range of subsequent behavioural possibilities. *Indeed, if freedom is taken as freedom from constraints, such a situation can only exist in a state of total disorder, or entropy. As order develops, constraints build up and freedom is thereby reduced. In the case of human behaviour, decisions taken consciously are limited by a number of more general decisions, taken unconsciously at different neurological levels. The whole pattern of 'decisions' made by an individual is itself limited by 'decisions' that have been taken ontogenetically, which in turn are limited by decisions made phylogenetically, while all of these decisions will be subject to social, ecological, biological, chemical and physical constraints, whose observance enables the individual to fulfil his role within the biosphere. Our behaviour is in fact limited by a whole hierarchy of constraints and the notion of freedom is largely illusory.*

### The Mind

The mind is yet another postulate whose possession is supposed to distinguish man from other animals. Held to be of a spiritual or non-material nature, its interaction with the crude world of matter is clearly very puzzling, at least for those who insist on maintaining a dualism of this sort.

To explain this apparent paradox, philosophers have worked out various theories, the best known of which are the theory of psycho-physical parallelism, where the twin domains run side by side without actually interfering with each other; the theory of interaction, whereby there is constant interaction between them, as the name implies; and, thirdly, that of identity, whereby we assume that both refer to a third and ultimate reality.

The concept of 'mind' is of use in a scientific context to the extent that it can serve as a variable of an objective model. We have seen that behaviour is explicable in terms of a control mechanism interacting with its environment (internal and external). If the term 'mind' is to be made use of as a variable in a scientific model of behaviour, I think it can best be regarded as a particular type of cybernism, and to be understood must be seen in the light of cybernisms in general, such as the nucleus that mediates the behaviour of a cell, or the genes that control the ontogenetic process. As soon as we use the term 'mind' in this way, the dichotomy between mind and matter automatically disappears. To begin with, the environment, which is in interaction with the cybernism, is itself made up of a hierarchical organisation of sub-cybernisms. More specifically, the body is made up of units such as cells, molecules, atoms, each of which has its own little 'mind', in which information is also organised, from which instructions are also transmitted, and which also provides a model of its specific system.

In fact, the relationship between the mind and the body can be regarded as a form of transduction. Information expressed in the medium of the cybernism is transduced into the medium of the sub-system. This is very much the same as saying that the environment is organised in accordance with instructions transmitted by and contained in the cybernism. Regarding it in this way also emphasises the essential fact that information is organised in the cybernism in that way *which will most favour the mediation of the optimum behaviour pattern.*

This point is perhaps best illustrated by the process of protein synthesis, involving the transduction of the information expressed in the medium of the genes into those enzymes that will determine the growth of the sub-system during ontogenesis.

This process was first described by Quick, Griffiths and Orgel.[112] An enzyme is a very large protein molecule. It consists of hundreds of amino-acid units arranged in a chain in a very specific order. This does not occur haphazardly, but must be determined by a corresponding set of instructions. The latter are transmitted by the genes.

**Instinct and Intelligence**
Among those features of man that are supposed to differentiate him from other animals is the intelligence. For a long time, this was considered to be a special faculty, which only men possessed, whereas the behaviour of other animals could be explained in terms of blind instinct. Even Fabre[113], who spent his life in minutely observing the nuances of insect behaviour, refused to accept that the many instances of discriminatory behaviour that he recorded could be classified as intelligent. Since they could not be attributed to the workings of 'blind instinct', he found it necessary to coin the term 'discernment'.

With the development of the discipline of ethology, intelligence has been grudgingly accepted as characterising, to some degree at least, the behaviour of non-human primates, and even animals of less exalted status. In spite of this, the dichotomy between intelligence and instinctive behaviour persists in the minds of all save the most enlightened, and is still a weapon in the armoury of those who wish to perpetuate the dualism between man and other animals. Let us examine the meaning of these terms.

Whether a behavioural response is said to constitute a tropism, a reflex, an instinctive act, or an intelligent one, it must be mediated by a hierarchical organisation of instructions, and differentiated at each step in accordance with environmental requirements. It is clear that these different types of behaviour differ from each other, but they do so in 'degree' rather than in 'kind'. As behaviour develops, the system involved becomes capable of reacting more and more adaptatively to increasingly more improbable environmental situations. This requires the development of a cybernism displaying ever greater complexity. Thus simple forms of life such as the dionaea flytrap or the sitaris beetle are only capable of the most rudimentary discrimination between the various constituents of their respective environments, and have a correspondingly low capacity for individual survival. The stickleback is capable of more discriminatory behaviour. Yet, during the mating season, the female will respond sexually to any red object, including the male stickleback, who adopts this colour at such a period, but also including such things as red balls or red lollipops. [114] A dog's powers of discrimination are very much higher than those of the stickleback, yet the animal will only be able to distinguish between legitimate visitors to its master's house, such as a delivery man, and less legitimate ones, such as a cat-burglar, after repeated experiences. Needless to say, man's discriminatory abilities are the highest of all, and his chances of individual survival are thereby maximised. The corresponding development of cybernismic organisation is confirmed neurophysiologically. At each stage in the phylogenetic process, the nervous system becomes progressively more centralised; the brain grows larger and larger, and more and more of the animal's actions become dependent on it. Thus, if one extracts the brain of a frog, it is still capable of a number of adaptive responses. It can move its leg, for instance, if pricked with a pin. A cat, however, after its brain has been extracted, is quite immobilised, and does not survive very long, whereas a man dies almost immediately.

Is there any radical jump in the course of this process that can be regarded as a frontier between distinct forms of behaviour? The answer is undoubtedly no. There is no reason to suppose that the human nervous system differs from that of its closest relations in the animal world in any radical manner. All that one can say is that the process of encephalisation and, in particular, encorticalisation, are more advanced.

The ratio of brain size to body size was considered very important in determining the relative 'intelligence' of different forms of life. Undoubtedly, the number of connections between neurons or groups of neurons is theoretically more significant, but, nevertheless, the former criterion provides a good indication of intellectual ability. If we apply it, we find that man does indeed obtain a higher rating than his nearest rivals, the ratio being four times higher in the case of a man than in that of a gorilla. On the other hand, it is roughly twenty times higher in the case of a gorilla than it is in that of a bird.[114] This fact is also indicative of the impossibility of establishing a frontier between man and other forms of life on the basis of intelligence.

If learning ability be regarded as a critrion of intelligence, then this conclusion is further confirmed. As Harlow [115] writes:

"The existing scientific data indicate a greater degree of intellectual communality among primates, and probably a greater communality among all animals, than has been commonly recognised. There is no scientific evidence of a break in learning capabilities between primate and non-primate forms. Emergence from the ocean to the land produced no sudden expansion of learning ability. Indeed, there is no evidence that any sharp break ever appeared in the evolutionary development of the learning process.

"That this is probably true should surprise no one. Indeed, the fundamental unity of learning and the continuity of its developing complexity throughout phylogenesis, or at least within the development of many major branches of the evolutionary tree, would seem to be in keeping with modern genetic theory."

In functional terms, one can consider that man is still in possession of that hierarchical organisation of instructions that we may refer to as his 'instincts', and that once determined the behaviour of our remote proto-hominid ancestors. All that has happened is that, as the result of the development of the brain, and in particular of the cerebral cortex, *these instructions can now be applied with greater precision and can thereby give rise to behaviour displaying a very much higher degree of stability.*

To conclude: the intelligence is not a new cybernismic mechanism that replaces, in any way, those that were previously operative, it is *merely the ability of the latter to operate in a more discriminatory manner and hence give rise to behaviour displaying higher stability.*

## The Ability to Transform the Environment
It is often maintained that humans can be distinguished from other animals by their ability to transform their environment to suit their purposes. However, a little reflection will show that this faculty is by no means

peculiar to humans; on the contrary, it is a feature of all organisms at whatever level of complexity. Indeed, among animal societies there are instances of this phenomenon which are just as impressive as those accomplished by human societies.

For instance, a termite's nest is a greater feat of engineering than is a sky-scraper in Manhattan, if the criterion used is the relative size of the builder and the building. The same can probably be said of the dams and canals built by beavers.

Among yet simpler animals, perhaps the most impressive example is the building of coral atolls in the tropical seas by minute polyps. The former often attain a very considerable size, as in the case of the Island of Zanzibar.

In direct contrast to the radical way in which such animal societies have modified their environment is the failure of certain primitive human societies such as those of the Australian aborigines to affect their environment in any way whatever. Stanner[116] writes:

"There are, of course, nomads, hunters and foragers who grow nothing, build nothing and stay nowhere long. Even in areas which are so inhabited it takes a knowledgeable eye to detect their recent presence. Within a matter of weeks, the roughly cleared camp sites may be erased by sun, rain and wind. After a year or two there may be nothing to suggest that the country was ever inhabited. Until one stumbles on a few old flint tools, a stone quarry, a shell midden, a rock painting, or something of the kind, one may think the land had never known the touch of man. They neither dominate their environment nor seek to change it."

### Social Behaviour Patterns
Human societies appear unique with respect to the elaborate and specialised societies they have evolved to adapt to the extraordinarily varied environments to which they have been submitted.

However, a glance at the adaptive capacity of ant societies reveals that this uniqueness is illusory. The nomadic and pillaging hordes of the Eurasian Steppe, such as the Huns and the Mongols, find their counterpart in the soldier or driver ants organised in hordes of 100,000 to 150,000 strong, who march out in perfect formation from their temporary bivouacs leaving a trail of destruction in their wake.[117]

Pastoral societies such as the Masai and the Navaho have their counterparts in those of the yellow lawn ants, who, in underground galleries, milk their herds of large aphid flies for the rich honey dew that they secrete.

The pygmies, who have adapted to life in the thick tropical forests, have their counterpart in the primitive and stunted Ponerine ants, who, driven by more successful species, eke out a precarious livelihood beneath

93

the surface of the soil.

The agricultural societies out of which our modern world has evolved have their counterparts in those of the famous grain-harvesting ants of the genus *Messor*, who meticulously collect millet or wheat, which is laid out in the sun to dry, the outer husk being split by the soldiers who then store it in well-drained chambers; or by the even more scientific ants, *Atta*, who cultivate (Rhozite) mushrooms that would normally grow to a gigantic size but which, by repeated cropping and replanting in carefully fertilized plantations, are never allowed to grow beyond the requisite height.

The hunting and food-gathering societies of the Australian Aborigines or the Bushmen have their counterpart in the carnivorous *Stigmatomma Pallipes*, who set out to track down underground game which they kill with the aid of their powerful sting.

Militarists such as the Assyrians and the Spartans find their counterpart in the blood-red slave-making ant, *formica sanguinea*, whose assaults on neighbouring nests for the purpose of seizing larvae to be brought up as salves, involve veritable military sieges with the despatch of reconnaissance parties, followed by a perfect blockade of all possible exits and a fierce direct onslaught via the most vulnerable approaches.

Medieval feudal society finds its counterpart in that of the slave-making ant, *Polyergus*, whose fierce sickle-jaws are so ill adapted to doing anything but crush the heads of his victims that he is no longer even able to feed himself. His military expeditions to capture his now indispensable slaves involve massive concerted attacks in which the whole army will charge as one unit on their unhappy victims.

The decadent societies of the Ottoman Sultanate and the Abbasid Caliphate have their counterpart in those of the slave-maker, *Strogyalanthus Huberi*, who is not only economically sustained by a large slave population, but also uses slaves as soldiers to conduct his wars. This parasitical ant is as vulnerable as was his human counterpart, for, as the result of many millenia of disuse, the muscles of his proud mandibles have atrophied, rendering them useless save as symbols of past glories, with which this pathetic figure, as helpless as he is awesome, can still hope to intimidate his gullible victims.[118]

## Culture

A persistent myth among reductionist scientists is that human cultural behaviour is of a totally different nature from any other type of behaviour, and cannot be subjected to scientific examination.

Indeed, the idea that writing symphonies, listening to string quartets, going to art exhibitions, indulging in small talk at cocktail parties, displaying kindness to one's neighbours, contributing to charities, etc., can be explained in terms of the same general behavioural model that also describes digestion, respiration and locomotion, and, even worse, the behaviour of lower forms of life such as fiddler crabs and dung beetles, is totally incompatible with man's elevated view of himself, and even the most enlightened thinkers of recent times have found it impossible to accept this fact. An example is von Bertalanffy,[119] who writes:

"Life and behaviour are not simply utilitarian, trying to come to a so-called equilibrium with minimum expense of physical and psychic energy. This is not even true of organic evolution, which often produces fantastic formations, behaviour patterns, colours, and what not, far exceeding mere survival and economic principles of adaptation. It is even less true of man, where, not by the wildest flight of fancy, can the creativity of an artist, musician or scientist be reduced to psychological and social adjustments, nor can the self-sacrifice of a martyr be reduced to the principle of utility. The whole human culture, whether Greek tragedy, Renaissance art or German music, simply has nothing to do with biological values of maintenance, survival, adjustment, or homeostasis. So far as the idea of any necessary progress of humanity is concerned (the human analogue to the biological concept of evolution), any criticism in our time of atomic warfare and a return to medieval techniques of statecraft would be an anachronism. In fact, the answer to our quest is very simple. Man, as the old saying goes, is a denizen of two worlds. He is a biological organism with the physical equipment, drives, instincts, and limitations of his species. At the same time, he creates, uses, dominates, and is dominated by, a higher world which, without theological and philosophical implications and in behavioural terms, can best be defined as the universe or universes of symbols. This is what we call human culture; and values, esthetic, scientific, ethical, religious — are one part of this symbolic universe. This is what man tries to achieve beyond satisfaction of his biological needs and drives; in turn, it governs and controls his behaviour."

Von Bertalanffy is in fact saying that cultural behaviour cannot be explained in objective terms. He is establishing a rigid dualism between this type of behaviour and all others, and this we know to be quite unjustified.

Let us look a little more closely into this particular form of the dualistic fallacy.

It is customary to regard cultural behaviour as behaviour that is 'learnt', as opposed to 'innate'. We might perhaps ask, what do we mean by 'learnt'? To this, Pringle[120] provides the best answer I have seen so far:

"Learning is the name given to the general class of processes by which

95

the behaviour of an animal comes to depend not only on the environmental changes immediately preceding it in time, but also on events which have occurred in the related parts of the environment in the more remote past. Students of animal behaviour distinguish this past into two parts: that period of past time during which the animal has existed as an independent organism, and the rest of past time during which its ancestors have existed. The modification of present behaviour by past events is called learning when those events have occurred *during the lifetime of the individual*, and instinct *when the events have occurred outside this period of time*. In the former case, the past events are supposed to have left some trace in the animal (usually in the nervous system), whereas in the latter case the organisation of the animal responsible for the observed response is supposed to be innate; that is, to be contained fully in the material substance of its inheritance . . .''

If the word 'learning' is to have any meaning, it cannot be limited to one particular set of modifications, to the exclusion of all others. From this it must follow that cultural behaviour, in the sense of behaviour 'learnt' neurogenetically cannot be regarded apart from that which was learnt phylogenetically and ontogenetically, and if the former are functional and adaptive, and hence can be studied scientifically, then so must the latter. I have shown that development, rather than constitute a continuous process, proceeds by a series of jumps, which occur as successive levels of complexity are reached. Each time, new principles are required to explain the new type of organisation that thereby comes into being. We have seen that behaviour is cumulative. These principles, therefore, do not replace those operative at the previous level, but merely supplement them. Thus a biological organism is explicable in terms of biology, but also continues to observe the laws of chemistry and physics, etc.

There is no reason to suppose that when we reach the level of complexity of the human society the jump involved is of a different nature from the previous ones, nor that the new discipline that thereby comes into being is distinguished from those that it complements in any radical manner.

Thus a society is explicable in terms of the laws slowly being evolved by sociologists and anthropologists, but nevertheless continues to obey those of biology, chemistry and physics, and all such disciplines have in common the fact that they are instances of the application of objective method to explaining behaviour at different levels of complexity.

### Cultural Adaptation in Non-Human Animals

The question might also be asked whether man is alone capable of cultural behaviour? Undoubtedly not. One can argue teleonomically from the fact that in many species, animals are subjected to a reasonably long period of parental tutelage to the hypothesis that cultural and not just genetic information must be transmitted from generation to generation. Thus Haldane[121] remarks that whereas the blackbird (*turdis merula*) has no cultural tradition, since males brought up in isolation will sing a perfect song, the skylark and chaffinch, on the other hand, must learn theirs. Reared in isolation, the skylark's song is apparently unrecognisable, and that of the chaffinch very imperfect. Thorpe has even noted different dialects among chaffinches. He found that he could recognise five different local chaffinch dialects in Great Britain. The chaffinches of the Azores, on the other hand: "... sing a dialect differing from any of the British dialects far more than they differ from one another."[122]

If their song is learned, as it appears to be, and if different groups use different dialects, it is clear that we can talk quite legitimately of the transmission of cultural matter from one generation to the next. Haldane also points out that there are examples among animal societies of the transmission of material objects from one generation to another. A good example is that of the agricultural ant, *atta*, who "... transmits pieces of the fungus 'rhozites' which they cultivate. Each piece is carried in a special cavity near the mouth and deposited in the new fungus garden."[121]

Other behavioural elements are also transmitted in the same manner. Haldane cites Kuo[123], whose experiments showed that cats would not generally kill mice or rats unless taught to do so by their parents. That this is so among lions and tigers is well documented.

There is a growing literature on the subject of social deprivation, among the higher animals in particular, which tends to confirm the thesis that its victims are thereby rendered incapable of fulfilling many of the necessary functions that make up their behavioural patterns.

Cultural innovation also appears to be a feature of non-human animal societies. Haskins[124] shows how the Argentine ant, *iridiomyrmex humilis*, abandoned an agricultural culture in favour of one permitting it to exploit the vast food potential of human habitations.

Haldane refers to the 'invention' among the great tits (*parus major*) of opening milk bottles that have been left on human doorsteps, which, having become common in England, has now spread to Holland; whether, as Haldane remarks: "... by cultural diffusion or by independent invention we know not."[121]

Indeed, though culture plays a greater role in the behaviour of man than in that of non-human animals, it is by no means a negligible factor in the latter and cannot constitute a barrier to their representation by the same general behavioural model.

# A Note on Directivity

All behavioural processes must be taken as being directive. I prefer this term to the term 'purposive', which in fact means the same thing. When we talk of somebody's purpose, we are not thinking of the role he plays within some general system, but rather of his 'conscious' motivation. If man's behaviour is determined by a mysterious supernatural force called the 'free will', then 'purpose' refers to the direction in which the exercise of 'free will' is leading him, and in terms of which his behaviour can be explained. Since animals other than men are supposed to be governed by 'blind instinct', they are not capable of exercising 'free will', and thus of displaying 'purposive' behaviour.

Even if we use the word 'purpose' teleonomically, its old metaphysical connotation still tends to linger. If we use it, for instance, in connection with the behaviour of such lowly animals as sea-urchins or fiddler crabs, subconsciously we cannot help but imagine these humble creatures consulting their little 'wills' before deciding 'freely' which zoo-planktons to have for tea. As this is not the image that I wish to convey, it is clearly easier to abandon the term 'purposiveness' altogether, in favour of one with no such undesirable connotation, i.e. directivity.

To deny directivity is in fact to deny that processes can be the object of scientific study. In spite of this, empiricists obstinately persist in so doing. This is partly due to the fact that they tend to regard three-dimensional things and one-dimensional processes apart, as though they were self-sufficient units. It is not currently realised that these units are nothing more than anthropocentric abstractions, neuro-cybernismic and linguistic units, but not units of the world they represent. There are no such things as dogs that do not eat and drink and reproduce, except as photographs, pictures, concepts and words, nor are there such processes as eating, drinking, breathing and reproducing taken apart from the organisms involved.

It follows that it simply does not make sense to discuss whether an animal's behaviour pattern can be 'inferred' from its physical form or not.

*The animal will eat and drink and breathe and reproduce because these processes are as much part of the animal as are the organs that permit these functions.*

*To deny directivity is to deny that cybernismic order can be put into dynamic processes, and hence that they can be subjected to scientific examination, and, since all the constituents of the world display different degrees of dynamism, that science itself is in fact possible.*

Empirically, the evidence of directivity is so overwhelming at all levels of complexity that its denial seems very naive. De Beer writes:

"The structure of an animal shows a number of exquisitely delicate adjustments: the splinters inside a bone are situated exactly where they are required to withstand the pressure to which the bone is subjected; the fibres of the tendon lie accurately along the line of strain between the muscle and the bone to which it is attached; centres of nerve cells in the brain are situated close to the ends of the nerve fibres, from which they habitually receive impulses, and when in phylogeny there is a change in the nerve fibres from which any given nerve-centre habitually receives its impulses, the nerve-centre is found to be situated near its new source of stimulation."[125]

Bierens de Haan makes the same point:

". . . that the weaving of the web by the spider is purposeful for the catching of insects, and the collecting and storing of caterpillars by the wasp purposeful for the nourishing of its future larvae, are facts that are so self-evident that it is not necessary further to elucidate them."[83]

The empirical evidence that is occasionally mustered to oppose the notion of directivity consists of examples of the behaviour of a system that are ostensibly contrary to its personal interests, but that, if examined more closely, are seen to be in the interest of the larger system of which it is part. *Indeed, if a sub-system is regarded in vacuo, its behaviour may not appear directive. If it is regarded as it should be, as a differentiated part of a larger system, its directivity then becomes apparent.*

Thus, for instance, it is argued that during the mating season the male stickleback undergoes colour changes that render him conspicuous and hence more vulnerable to predators. It has been shown that the object of the colour change is to attract the attention of females. That the stickleback has enemies who have learned to take advantage of this conspicuousness (as the predator's behaviour is also directive) is only to be expected and does not detract from the directive nature of its colour change for breeding purposes.[114] The latter remains adaptive so long as the breeding advantages outweigh the disadvantages for the purposes of phylogeny.

An infinite number of examples of the same principle can be cited, thus:

Certain fish learn to tolerate smaller fish that enter their mouths and clean their teeth. This is known as 'cleaning symbiosis'. However, predators have 'learned' to imitate these cleaners, and have grown to look exactly like them. They are consequently tolerated by the larger fish, a fact they take advantage of by taking an occasional bite at their unsuspecting hosts.[126]

In many species of ants, specialised workers have evolved to look after the larvae. Certain cuckoo-like parasitic beetles, incapable of looking after their own larvae, lay their eggs in the ants' nests. These later hatch into larvae that are indistinguishable from the ants' and which, after having been carefully looked after by the workers, hatch into predator beetles that gradually take over the colony.[117]

These are but two of an infinite number of examples of parasites that take advantage of certain features of a host's behaviour pattern. Does this mean that these features are not directive? Undoubtedly not. It is clear that cleaning symbiosis is very useful to the host; it is also clear that looking after the larvae is a necessary function within an ant colony and is essential for the survival of the young. The fact that, for these functions to occur successfully, a number of individual members of the species must fall prey to parasites is no argument against their usefulness.

A broody hen, for instance, will sacrifice her life if necessary to protect her chicks against predators. Individual members of social communities, such as driver ants, will also sacrifice their lives in the interest of their societies, just as individual members of human societies will lay down their lives in the interest of a larger group to which they belong, whether a community or a religious sect.

Such behaviour only appears non-directive if we regard the individual *in vacuo*, i.e. apart from the family or the community of which he is a part.

Again, it is pointed out that the fierce competition obtaining in certain animal societies for the possession of the choicest female or of the most desirable territory is not conducive to the individual survival of the competitors. Indeed, in such competitive societies as those of the baboons or fur seals, casualties can often run quite high. But such behaviour can only be interpreted as contributing to the selection of the fittest individuals and thus to the adaptation of the species as a whole to the challenge of its environment.

Professor Wynne-Edwards[127] has collected much information in favour of this thesis that such competition is the most important advantage to be derived from animal agglomerations. I have already pointed to the role of competition in establishing social order. The error lies once more in taking the individual as the unit rather than the species as a whole.

It is occasionally also pointed out that in certain species the individual, at one or more stages during its life-cycle, is subjected to so many environmental challenges that its chances of survival are in fact minute. This is especially the case with certain parasites. Miriam Rothschild and Teresa Clay[128] write:

". . . the eggs of the grouse round worm lie scattered all over Scotland, but millions and millions of their young, which hatch out and wriggle up the sprigs of heather around them, perish because that particular plant is never eaten by a grouse. Similarly, vast numbers of immature ticks cling hopefully to blades of grass, waiting for the millionth chance which will bring an animal brushing through the vegetation within reach of their waving forelegs.

"Owing to the difficulty of finding a host — a difficulty which is superimposed on the more familiar hazards of life — the mortality among most parasites is enormous. A vast number of larvae have to be produced in order that the species can survive at all. Consequently, a characteristic feature of most parasites is a relatively enormous development of the reproductive organs, which frequently come to dominate the body. Intestinal worms produce eggs by the million and even brood-parasites like the cuckoo lay four or five times as many eggs as their hosts. The difficulty of host-finding can often be estimated by the number of eggs laid."

Surely nothing could be more directive than this automatic regulation of the number of eggs laid in accordance with the number required to produce the minimum number of adults. Once again, directivity is apparent if one realises that the unit of analysis must be the species and not the individual.

Other arguments against directivity are based on the disadvantages to individual survival of the so-called inflexibility of instinctive behaviour. Thus Hingston[129] tells of a clubionide spider in Central India. These spiders live in grassy meadows. They are the same colour as the grass and are capable of lying in a particular position that enables them to blend perfectly with their background. When threatened, their instinct is to remain perfectly immobile and thus hope to pass unnoticed. Hingston found that, in such circumstances, there was no way to make them move, neither by pushing them with a straw, by sticking a pin into them, nor even by cutting off one of their legs. They would inevitably remain quite immobile.

Canis azarae, the pampas fox, apparently behaves in a similar way. Can one say that its behaviour is not directive? Undoubtedly not. From the point of view of the species, it must constitute the reaction most conducive to survival.

A further example is that of the phenomenon of blinking. The human eyelid closes to prevent a foreign particle from entering the eye. The performance of this task suffers from the same shortcomings as does the Dionaea fly-trap. It cannot distinguish between the various foreign particles, most of which are harmful, but some of which could conceivably be beneficial, such as the medicinal drops which an occulist may wish to insert into a diseased eye. Does this detract from the usefulness of the blinking function? The answer is no. The experience of phylogeny has established that, statistically, blinking, like digestion and the circulation of the blood, are best dealt with without the intervention of conscious or 'intelligent' behaviour. The possibility that a foreign particle entering the eye might be beneficial is so remote that it is best not taken into account. The cost of doing so, in terms of the increase in the size of the population of neurons required for increasing discrimination, would not make it worthwhile. Indeed, in spite of the elated view we may have of human intelligence, it is probable that if this faculty were allowed to govern all those elaborate processes necessary to sustain life, which are at present mediated by lower centres in our spinal cord, the result would undoubtedly be a serious increase in inefficiency. Blinking may appear indiscriminatory, but this lack of discrimination is a low price to pay for the advantages of automatism and for the protection it enjoys from the ravages of 'intelligent' behaviour that is at present wreaking such irreparable damage to the less well protected parts of the biosphere.

# The Directivity of Cultural Behaviour

Cultures do not develop at random but in an orderly manner like all other behavioural processes. As Murdock writes: "Culture is adaptive or functional, sub-serving the basic needs of its carrier and altering through time by a sort of mass trial and error in a process which is truly evolutionary, i.e., characterised by orderly adaptive change."[130]

The function of culture at the social level of complexity is precisely the same as that of the personality at the level of the individual. A culture develops as a response to a specific, in this case, long-term, environmental situation. We know that a sub-system cannot be examined *in vacuo*, but as part of a system. Remove the particular environment to which the sub-system or its behaviour pattern is an adaptation, and the latter loses its *raison d'être* and will simply atrophy. Modify the environment, and clearly the behaviour pattern must be correspondingly modified.

This is illustrated by Kardiner in his discussion of Comanche culture.[69] The Comanches had a cultural behavioural pattern that was optimum for a hunting and food-gathering people living in a relatively arid environment. After the arrival of the white man, this environment was modified in many ways. In particular, there were migrations of other Indian tribes, and the horse made its appearance. To these new conditions, the Comanches reacted by slowly developing a 'bandit' culture, living by preying on their more civilised neighbours. This was reflected in a corresponding change in their culture. Thus the most prestigious figure was no longer the medicine man but the war chief. The attitude to the aged changed. Previously, infanticide had been practised, as among most food-gathering peoples. Children now became more valuable, and the adoption of children from neighbouring tribes to be brought up as warriors increased. The ghosts were far less feared, since they now had real enemies to fulfil the same function. The sun dance, originally connected with masochistic and self-destructive rituals, played a less important role as much better outlets for these psychological requirements were now available. The notion of *mana*, or power, which was fundamental to the Comanche model of the world, began to be attached less to property and became transmissible from man to man and pooled by the group. There was a decline in the fear of the dead. The old rituals involving the burning of a dead man's property slowly fell into disuse. In general, a new culture developed which was highly adaptive to the new circumstances in which they lived. However, when the environmental conditions were once more radically transformed, this time as the result of the confinement of this warlike tribe to the shelter of a reservation, its cultural pattern totally disintegrated.

As Kardiner writes: "The society could exist only as long as there were slaves to steal, cattle to rustle; in other words, the fine ego-structure of the Comanches was bought at the expense of criminality perpetuated on others at the cost of the complete collapse of the society once this criminality was incapable of being exercised. No internal growth or expansion of the society was possible. The results of acculturation of the Comanches bears this out. When they were returned under Government protection, the culture continued to exist largely in the memories of the old men. The children became less important, no feasts were given in their honour. The sexual development was given free range. The aged again became important, because the young could perform no exploits to compare with them. The status of the old was further advanced by the creation of vested interests."[69]

The same thing happened to the pastoral Navahos once they were deprived of their cattle. At first sight, the symptoms of cultural breakdown could be attributed to a fall in their standard of living. That this was not primarily so is shown by Simpson: "With the decline in livestock holdings came a necessary decline in certain types of behaviour viewed as desirable by the Navahos. Kin did not fulfil their obligation to kin, neighbours to neighbours, rich to poor, because the wherewithal for reciprocity and generosity was no longer there. There was a pervasive feeling that people did not behave as they should, or as they once did, and this I would call a deprivation in the area of behaviour."[131]

Aberle considers that the loss of livestock holdings among the Navaho was one of the principal causes of that revolutionary messianic cult known as Peyotism, which developed shortly afterwards: "The Peyote cult, with its protesting ideology and adjusting ethic, 'made sense' to people whose traditional culture could no longer operate effectively, and who were forced to accommodate to the new situation."[132]

It is the realisation that cultural traits are directive and adaptive that leads to the notion of a culture as a control mechanism and of the society that it controls as a natural system whose behaviour is subjected to the same laws as that of all other natural systems. This sort of thinking is also giving rise to the vital new discipline of cultural ecology.

# Cultural Convergence

The early ethnographers were mainly struck by exotic cultural divergences. Slowly, with the development of scientific method, the accent has shifted to the study of the much more impressive similarities that characterise the cultural patterns of peoples occupying similar ecological niches. These were originally attributed to cultural contacts, or diffusion. Such a thesis is no longer entertained by serious anthropologists, since similar cultural traits can be shown to have developed independently by people inhabiting different continents, isolated by oceans, mountain ranges, and other natural barriers, and who could have had no possible contact in historical times.

Striking examples are the extraordinary prevalence of the concept of power, or vital force, in the world-view of primitive peoples, and the role played by ancestor worship in their 'religious' practices. Regarding the latter, it appears to have characterised, to a greater or lesser degree, the beliefs and practices of peoples at a certain stage of cultural development. Thus we find it among the Australian aborigines, the Indians of North and South America, the peoples of India and South East Asia, and both the Chinese and Japanese. Lods[40] tells us that it was the original religion of the Jews , Karsten[133] that of the Empire of the Incas, Fustel de Coulanges[6] that of the ancient Greeks, and Robertson Smith[45] that of the ancient Semites.

We are led to a similar conclusion by an examination of magical practices and of the different rituals that punctuate the life-cycle of man in simple societies. Thus, initiation ceremonies appear to be common to all peoples, and they very often take very similar forms. Among these, circumcision appears to be common to peoples as distant from each other as the Australian aborigines and the ancient Egyptians. The notion that during circumcision the initiate is swallowed by a large monster, who vomits him back to life, after which traumatic event the child qualifies as an adult of the tribe, is, according to Vergiat,[134] common to the Urbunnas of Central Australia, the Anulas of the Gulf of Carpentaria, the Bukanas of New Guinea, the Sulkas of New Brittany, as well as to many other peoples of Australia, Oceania, and Africa, such as the Bushmen of the Kalahari and the Manja of Ubangi. Kenyatta[73] points to the existence of this same belief among the Kikuyu and related tribes.

The study of social structures reveals astonishing similarities in those developed by peoples at the same level of complexity, and fulfilling similar ecological niches in totally distinct areas of the world. Bilateral extended families, unilateral clans that may be patrilineal or matrilineal, rules of residence that may be patrilocal or matrilocal, strict laws of exogamy and endogamy, age-grades, secret societies, military societies, etc., are to be found among people as remote from each other as the Amer-Indians, the Bantu, and the Australian aborigines. Indeed, as Murdock writes: "Any structural forms can be developed anywhere if conditions are propitious."[22]

The same is true of religious systems. Similar myths, beliefs and religious practices are to be found among peoples between whom there can have been no possible cultural contact.

Gray points to a striking example of religious convergence: that between Christianity and the religion of the Sonjo of Northern Tanzania.[135] The latter are a Bantu people, who practise agriculture in a small area entirely surrounded by hostile Masai pastoralists. Their religion appears to diverge very radically from the African norm, in that the ancestral cult is relatively insignificant. Instead, they are principally concerned with the worship of their cultural hero, Khambageu, and have developed a cult which resembles Christianity in many ways. Khambageu was born, like Christ, in a supernatural way, apparently "through his father's swollen leg." Both Khambageu and Christ were humble men, worked miracles of healing, and died from maltreatment by the people — in Khambageu's case, as a result of overwork, as he was forced to work overtime to cure the sick. Both rose to heaven, and, in each case, their tombs were afterwards found empty. Once in heaven, both became identified with God, Khambageu with the sun god, Riob. In addition, the extension of divinity to the former's son, Aka, establishes a sort of trinity reminiscent of the Christian one. In both religions, we find a religious rite marking initiation into the ranks of the faithful: baptism in the case of Christianity, and the *ntemi* scar in the case of the cult of Khambageu. Both religions foresee the end of the world, and the return of their respective Messiahs to save the faithful.

Gray considers that the Sonjo religion was ". . . developed independently (of Christianity), perhaps during a time of crisis, brought on by the incursion of the Masai into the region."[135] Thus its similarity with Christianity cannot be explained in terms of cultural diffusion, and the two religions can only be regarded as adaptive reactions to similar systemic conditions, i.e., as very striking examples of cultural convergence.

Such religions undoubtedly began as Messianic cults. These seem to occur in periods of social disorder, after the breakdown of a cultural pattern, and their object is clearly to recreate a new one, more in keeping with changed systematic requirements. The literature on this subject is Lake among the Iroquois and that of Father Cicero in Brazil. These, revolutionary movements in the European Middle Ages that are normally classified as heresies. Vittorio Lanternari[137] shows how all the revolutionary cults developed by contact with the colonialist powers, are but variations around this same theme. The most famous among these are possibly the Peyote religion among the Navahos, the cargo cults among the Melanesians, Rastafarianism in Jamaica, the religion of Handsome Lake among the Iriquois and that of Father Cicero in Brazil. These, however, are only a few among tens of thousands of such movements. Wherever they occur, whether it be among the tribal societies of India, Pakistan, China, Africa, Australia, or Melanesia, they will have many similar features: their leaders will have in common certain psychological traits, their doctrines will appeal to the same frustrated psychological requirements, and the responses of their adepts will be characterised by the same pattern of naivity, self-sacrifice, and fanaticism. Lowie considers that a study of the Messianic cultures of primitive peoples provides ". . . an irrefutable proof that cultural traits can develop independently in distinct areas."[138]

*What is true of myths, social structures and religious movements, seems also to be true of all cultural traits, and hence of cultures as a whole. The latter in fact, can be regarded as long-term adaptive responses, which, like all other behavioural responses, can be understood in terms of the same general model of behaviour.*

# The Integrity of Cultural Behaviour

A culture like all cybernisms must be regarded as an integral whole. Cultural traits can only be examined in accordance with their function within the whole. They cannot be judged in isolation, nor can the criteria used for judging them be those of other cultures for which they were not designed, as has been done by missionaries and colonial administrators. The suppression of customs and institutions in simple societies that, judged by our particular standard of morality, may appear undesirable or even evil, can have fatal results on the cultures involved, very much as the extraction of specific organs from a body can result in its annihilation.

This principle is so important that it is well worth illustrating in detail.

If one is acquainted with the culture of any ordered society and is capable of working out the role played by each of the customs and institutions within this culture, i.e. by determining in what way they contribute towards the adaptive behaviour of the society to its particular environment, one can easily imagine what would be the consequences of their suppression by outside interference.

Let us take the case of the marital customs of the Comorians. [139] The people of the Comores have a complex social organisation, probably based on indigenous customs, upon which were superimposed those of their Islamic conquerors. From the former they inherited a matrilineal and matrilocal tradition, from the latter a patrilineal and patrilocal one. Islamic marital law has also been adopted. As a result, there is polygamy and a high frequency of divorce. Indeed, so high is the latter that it is perfectly normal for a woman to have been married five to ten times. From the experience gained in our culture, we would tend to associate such a consequent number of 'broken homes' with a very high rate of juvenile delinquency, schizophrenia, and suicide. However, things do not work out that way. In the Island of Mayotte, delinquency is unknown (1971). There are two schizophrenics out of a population of 30,000, and there have only been two murders in the last fifty years. The society has thus adapted itself to marital instability, which ours has not. The reasons are two-fold. Firstly, by virtue of the institution of matriliny and matrilocality, a child is partly the responsibility of the mother's clan. Many of the functions of fatherhood are in fact fulfilled by the mother's elder brother, and inheritance, for instance, is primarily through him rather than through the father. Secondly, by custom, the step-father automatically assumes many of the responsibilities of fatherhood, *vis-à-vis* the children that his new wife has had with previous husbands. The step-father, or *baba combo*, is, in particular, responsible for the payment of the very large expenses involved in the circumcision ceremony of his stepsons. Also, the father's role is reduced by the fact that the children are brought up in the mother's home. In addition, as the father probably has several other wives, he would in any case have only been physically present in one particular house on one or two days a week. For all these reasons, divorce does not have the same unsettling effect in the Comores that it does in our society. Now, supposing a busybody missionary or administrator suddenly decided that matriliny and matrilocality were vestiges of barbarity not to be found in modern advanced societies, and that they must therefore be abolished; unless he abolished at the same time many of the other customs making up this complex culture, the results would be disastrous. Schizophrenia, delinquency, and the other symptoms of social disorder would undoubtedly result, as they do in our society with the break-up of the nuclear family.

Another example can be drawn from the same people. When a woman is divorced by her husband, and before she can find a new one, she is deprived of all normal means of sustenance. The cattle and the fields belong to the husband. Only the house is hers. How, in these conditions, can she pay for her upkeep? The answer is that she is expected to have a lot of lovers, who must reward her financially for her favours. The more money a woman is capable of extracting from them, the more highly will she be regarded. Indeed, it appears that the greatest insult for a woman is to be told that she sleeps with men for nothing. This custom may appear particularly repugnant to those imbued with what remains of the values of our disintegrating society, yet it is considered absolutely normal in the Comores, and to abolish it would clearly lead to disastrous results. Indeed, unless a profound modification were brought about to the matrimonial system and property-owning customs of the Comorians, in which this type of 'prostitution' plays an essential part, there would be no means for a divorced woman to support herself.

Indeed, to judge the customs of primitive people by applying socio-centric criteria *in vacuo* and then seeking to abolish those that conflict with the specialised set of values underlying our cultural pattern is very much like considering an animal deformed if its physical features differ from our own, and engaging a plastic surgeon to recast them in our likeness, regardless of any adaptive function they might fulfil within a particular behaviour pattern.

Malinowski expressed the notion of the integrity of cultures thus:

"When we come to the integral institutions of a tribe or a nation, matters become extremely complicated. And the reason for this is that an important institution like the family or chieftainship, ancestor worship or agriculture has its roots in all aspects of culture. It is connected with so many cultural realities, some of which it is by no means easy to alter, that nothing except a complete transformation of the whole society can provide a painless change, free from maladjustments. Thus the African family, plus polygyny, plus matriliny, plus brideprice, could be replaced by a patriarchal, Christian family based on Roman Law, the Code Napoleon, or English Civil Law. But such a change could only be achieved by transforming the whole society simultaneously, and by giving the necessary wherewithal to establish the new and more elaborate type."[140]

What Malinowski does not say is that such a transformation would lead to a marked reduction in social stability.

# The Family Basis of
# Social Structure in Benin

JIMOH OMO FADAKA

---

The Edo people number about three million and they live in Bendel State, one of the 19 states of modern Nigeria. They are divided into different ethnic groups, the Binis, the Ishans, the Afenmais, the Urhobos, and the Ikas. They have much in common and speak very similar languages. Foremost among them are the Binis who are organised into the kingdom of Benin, where I come from.

Benin is famous throughout the world for its art, in particular its bronzes, the work of a caste of smiths. It was visited by Ibn Battuta in the Middle Ages, who gives a vivid description of the capital city.[141] Its independence came to an end in 1897 when the British expedition rased the city to the ground sending the Oba (king) into exile.

Bini history, however, has never been written down. The annals of the Obas, their wars and triumphs are transmitted orally from generation to generation, together with the customs and traditions of the Bini people.

### The Oba
The most important institution of Benin is the kingship. The Oba is the divine king, as was the pharaoh of Egypt, the king of the Akans, the Ashanti, and the Shilluk on the Nile, and the kings of the ancient Greeks in Homeric times.

Sir James Frazer has described in great detail what were the principles of divine kingship and these principles apply to the Oba of Benin.[142] The Oba is the custodian of Bini culture and also the high priest of the cult of his own ancestors, which is the national religion of Benin. It is also in his person that resides the power or vital force or 'mana', as the Polynesians call it, of the whole kingdom — the Etin-Oba as it is referred to in Benin. The survival of the kingdom is considered to hinge on the preservation of this power; if it is allowed to ebb, there is danger of natural calamities, floods, droughts, enemy invasion. On the other hand, if the right measures are taken to assure its preservation, then the society will prosper. We find the same notion in the Jewish Old Testament, when catastrophes of all sorts were attributed to the king's transgressions, in particular to his building graven images to live gods, i.e. breaking the society's most firmly entrenched taboos. To preserve the Etin-Oba, the Oba's behaviour must be subjected to a very exacting set of cultural constraints. One such constraint is that, during the Igue Festival held every year, he must not see any foreigners. It was his refusal to see a group of British traders on this important occasion, their refusal to take 'no' for an answer, and their subsequent intrusion into his palace that led to their massacre and to the punitive expedition of 1897.

The function of all national festivals is to renew Etin-Oba, and of these the most important is the Igue Festival. If the rituals performed during the national festivals renew the Etin-Oba, the breaking of a taboo surrounding the Oba's person reduces it. This explains why the violation of such a taboo is one of the two crimes that are punished by death.

If the Oba's power shows any signs of diminishing, he must immediately be replaced by a more vigorous successor. If it is the people's opinion that this is the case, then they will make this apparent during the Igue Festival and create disturbances or riots. If this occurs then the Oba must abdicate. In practice it has never yet occurred.[143]

## The Prime Minister and the Chiefs

The Oba rules through his Prime Minister, who is appointed for life, and a council composed of 15 chiefs. In theory the Oba has the power to dismiss the council or for that matter any of the chiefs who compose it, but in reality this has never happened. The Oba is a truly constitutional monarch.

Some of the social power or Etin also resides in the chiefs (Etin-Ogie). Like the power residing in the Oba, it must be renewed through special ceremonies, either at tribal or at village level.

## The Family

The family is the basis of Benin society. It is an economic, social, political and religious unit. It is economic in the sense that agricultural activities are carried out in family holdings, although co-operation will occur among groups of families at special times (harvest for instance). Traditional crafts are also family affairs, in that the necessary know-how is handed down from father to son.

The relationship between the members is laid down by custom. It has great cohesion and is held responsible for the performance of certain social functions, for instance the education of children born into it; also for the crimes committed by them until they have reached the age of ten. If a child breaks a taboo surrounding the person of the Oba, it is the parents who are held responsible. If a person wounds or even kills another, he must pay compensation to the latter's family. Marriage is also not only something which concerns two people; it is a contract between two families which links them together in all sorts of culturally determined ways.

The father is head of the family. He has great power over its members. This power he derives from his status as the head of the family, and from his position of priest of the cult of his family's ancestors. There is also power or Etin vested in the father and hence in the family (Etin-Eta). Ceremonies are carried out at family level to ensure the preservation of this power, whilst the violating of taboos likely to break it is scrupulously avoided. The Bini family is polygamous and includes members of several generations. It is what is normally referred to as an 'extended family'.[144]

## Settlement Patterns

The custom is for women to have their own huts in which they live with their children. The huts are arranged in a circle around the husband's hut. This does not mean that he will live alone; one or two of his wives will tend to be with him, possibly too his widowed mother or other female relatives.

If a man dies, his wife and children immediately become the responsibility of his eldest living brother. This means that one is also likely to find other female members of the family with their children in the settlement or compound — a divorced sister for instance. If a woman gets divorced, the property she inherited from her father is taken away from her husband and becomes hers again.

## The Village

The village is made up of several such compounds. The members of a village tend to be related to one another which makes co-operation among its members very much easier. The village is usually run by a village chief (to be distinguished from the advisory chiefs making up the Oba's council). The chief is not hereditary, but is elected for life by the villagers — in general, on the basis of his prestige and social service. The government of the village is democratic, every adult man being expected to take part. If he does not he is very much looked down upon. Each one of them has some practical role to play in the government of the village and each one can also be dismissed if he does not observe its established rules of conduct. There are no formal institutions. Everything is very informal, and at village meetings, all comments and ideas, however critical, are listened to, indeed encouraged. Usually unanimous agreement is obtained on important issues. When this is not possible, the majority decision is accepted by the opposing minority.[145]

## Land Tenure

Land is held by the head of the family, who acts as custodian on its behalf. When he dies, his eldest son divides the land up as he sees fit among his brothers and sisters. They too will hold it as custodians for their families. No land can be sold without the agreement of the whole family and this is very unlikely to be given. It is passed on from one generation to the next, contributing in this way to social and ecological stability.

If the Government wishes to acquire land for some development scheme, it must first get in touch with the village council, composed as we have seen of all the heads of families. The only way to get round the general reluctance on the part of families to sell their land is to lease it from them. In this way, they know that one day it will be theirs again and their status within the community is relatively unimpaired. It is impossible, however, for foreigners to acquire land in Benin.

## Clans

The Binis are divided up into five exogamous clans — that is to say, people may not marry within their clan. The clan is not a territorial unit, which means that people living in different villages will be linked together by virtue of being members of it. Yet it plays a very big part in Benin social life. This is because people are closely identified with their clans, perhaps as much as they are with their family and village. Some clans are prestigious, others are not. It is very much in a person's favour if he is a member of a prestigious clan. It is very much against him if he is a member of one that has little prestige. As a result, there is a good deal of competition between the clans so that they may increase their respective standing. Each clan is run by a chief, assisted by an elected council. Clans hold annual festivals which are very lavish affairs, when gifts are presented to the members of other clans who happen to reside in the same area. The clan's prestige is highly dependent on the lavishness of its ceremonies and the gifts given to other clans.

## Welfare

In times of hardship or crisis, any Bini can depend on help from his family or his clan. As we have already seen, widows are looked after by their husband's brother, while divorced women obtain possession of the property previously passed on by their father to their husband. In general, the extended family looks after any of its members who might be in need either temporarily or permanently. In addition, it is one of the functions of the clan to provide material help for its members. No clan wishes to see its members suffering material hardship, as its standing would be greatly reduced. The clan is thereby highly motivated to ensure the welfare of its members. In this way a Bini has a very great sense of security, which cannot be provided either by money or state welfare systems.[146]

## Crime Control

As already pointed out, if a child breaks a taboo its parents are held responsible and will be punished. If an adult breaks a taboo and the crime does not menace the security of the state, he must pay compensation to the victim's family. On the whole, however, there is very little crime in Bini society: this is because of the powerful social control exerted by public opinion. If a person's behaviour diverges from the expected norm, he is boycotted (bizu-gbe). No-one goes to his feasts and this is a terrible insult, so great in fact that few people are willing to take the risk of having it happen to them.

Among many African peoples, the persistent criminal is expelled from the tribe. He then loses his social status and becomes an isolate, which is the most terrible fate for anyone. Among the Binis, an isolate neither belongs to a family, nor a community, nor a clan and is referred to as an Azan. He is despised and feared, and children who don't behave themselves are threatened with the Azan, the bogey man, so to speak.

The death penalty is meted out to persistent criminals as it is to those who violate the taboo surrounding the Oba's person and threaten the security of the tribe as a whole.

## Education

There is no formal education in the sense in which we know it in the West. Children are educated by growing up. As this occurs, they pass through four different age groups. From zero to ten the child lives within the family unit and is subjected exclusively to parental influences; at the age of ten he enters another age grade, where he remains until he is twenty (during this period he learns to fulfil communal and tribal functions as well as family ones and is increasingly under the influence of his peer group). From the age of twenty to forty, if a boy, he becomes a warrior; it is by getting married, however, that a person really becomes an adult member of his society. Once a married man has reached the age of forty, and thereby become an elder, he can take part in the government of his village.

The purpose of Bini traditional education is to prepare the child for participation in the life of the community, the ideal of which is correct relations with, and behaviour towards, others. The communal organisation and educational system reinforces the principle that one's behaviour towards others is what matters most. The strength and number of social ties between members of the same family, clan and age group and between different families and clans means that the community can very easily be mobilised for co-operative activity. The building of houses, fences, bridges, cultivation and harvesting, even sowing, are usually group activities. The people know that if a job has to be done, they must do it together. Families and family groups work together to provide what they need.

## Religion

Religion plays a predominant role in the life of the Binis. It is totally enmeshed in their social activity, so much so that there is no true notion of religion as conceived in the West and no word for it in their vocabulary.

In Bini traditional religion, there is no official priesthood, nor is there any religious preaching. Converting 'pagans' or 'unbelievers' is a thing unknown. This is due to the fact that religion is interwoven with the tradition and social customs of the people. Thus all members of the community are automatically considered to have acquired, during their childhood, all that it is necessary to know about religion and custom. The duty of imparting this knowledge to children is entrusted to the parents who are looked upon as the official ministers of both religious and social customs.[147]

## Deity Worship

The Bini believe in one god, the creator and giver of all things. God has no father or mother or companions of any kind. His work is done in solitude. The Binis have no temples; they select huge trees, under which they worship and make sacrifices to God. These sacred trees are regarded in the same manner as most Christians regard churches, as the 'House of God'.

God is not visible to the mortal eye; he manifests himself in various ways: the sun, the moon, the stars, the rain, rainbows, lightning and thunder are looked upon as manifestations of his powers. Through these signs, he can reveal his love or hatred. For instance, when there is thunder and lightning, it is taken as a warning to clear the way for God's movement from one sacred place to another.

In the ordinary way of everyday life, there are no organised prayers or religious ceremonies, such as 'morning' or 'evening' prayers. So long as everything goes well, it is assumed that God is pleased with the general behaviour of the people and the welfare of the society. In this happy state there is no need for prayers.

Another aspect of Bini traditional religion remains. Inevitably, the people are daily and hourly in the most intimate contact with nature. We have already seen that certain natural phenomena, thunder and lightning, are regarded as direct manifestations of God and his works. He controls not only the health and lives of people and animals on whom people depend, but also rain and the supply of food which the rain brings from the soil. Hence all these phenomena of Nature are in some degree, like thunder, imbued with the spirit of God, and give rise to sacrificial practices. Any description of Bini traditional religion which left these out of account would be incomplete.

Binis do not speak of 'nature worship' as a separate part of their religion; it is a quality that runs through the whole, vitalising it and keeping in constant touch with daily need and emotions. Nor is there a distinction between the spiritual and the temporal. Religion is integrated into the whole of society's structure and is indistinguishable from other aspects of its activities.

Bini traditional religion can, therefore, be defined as being based on belief in a supreme being, God, and on constant communication with nature. To make use of European terminology, it might be said that religion in Benin is 'state established', but it would be even more true to say that church and state are one. Indeed, Benin religion is a social institution. It serves to sanctify the tribe's character and structure and hence to preserve it.[148]

### The Ancestors

Very important in the life of the Binis is the cult of their ancestors. When a man dies, he does not move to some distant heaven but remains part of his family, his village, his clan and his tribe. He remains therefore a member of Benin society. Ancestors, because they retain their social status, can be regarded as organised in the same way as is Benin society. Communion with them is carried out at the appropriate social level; thus communion with the ancestors of the Oba is carried out by the tribe as a whole, while the ancestors of the family are contacted by the family itself. In this sense, the Oba, the chief of the clan, and the head of the family are priests; they are the intermediaries with ancestral spirits at their particular social level, and all of them are responsible for performing the appropriate rituals and sacrifices by virtue of which the living must fulfil their obligations to the dead and thereby ensure their society's continuity.

There are certain crises in the life of a Bini, when he or she may require spiritual assistance: for example he may have broken a taboo, and attributed some ill luck to such an infraction. This is reckoned to be a personal matter, and God is not approached. The person's purification or absolution is achieved by means of the medicine man, who will work by establishing contact with such of the ancestral spirits as may be thought involved. It is possible that only one ancestor will need to be approached, and there is no need for the whole family group to be brought into action to approach him.

If a person falls sick, or has an injury, it is not at first a matter for God or supernatural treatment. Ordinary medical knowledge is applied. If this does not succeed, the nature of the case is changed. Then the ancestors are communicated with. With the aid of a diviner, it may then be found that one of the ancestors has been offended. Atonement is made and the invalid recovers. Yet even when it is certain that no ancestors remain offended, the illness may still not yield to the treatment. Then the father of the family must organise the next appeal to God through a sacrifice.

Now the living and the dead of the family together approach God. This assures God that the occasion is serious and that the whole family is indeed at one, having exhausted all other means, in pleading for his help. The living and the dead make the approach by means of a sacrificial ceremony which is essential in Bini religion. These two cases of an ordinary illness and of an injury throw light on the respective parts played in the actual lives of the people by God, worship, communion with ancestors and sacrificial practices or ceremonies. This demonstrates the essentially religious aspect of Benin social behaviour.[149]

### World View

Bini traditional religion takes a holistic view of nature, and the people live in harmony with nature and not against it. In the life of the Binis, the Earth is the mother of all things animate, and the generations are so closely linked together by their common participation in the land that agricultural ritual and reverence for ancestral spirits play the foremost part in religious activities. Family ties, kinship, ethnic and communal groupings are very strong.[150]

Even though Bini culture has survived British domination and other foreign influences, it has, since Independence, been subjected to serious strain by present economic developments. The result is that the people are becoming increasingly detached from their own social units and their own traditions. These changes have up till now appeared justified in narrow economic terms. They have given rise to an elite trained in the application of western technologies and to an urban proletariat available for work in factories and other large-scale commercial enterprises.

Few, however, realise what has been the human cost. The ignorance displayed by the majority of our politicians as to the true nature of the cultural patterns of so-called primitive peoples has not enabled them to appreciate their extraordinary value, both in human and even in economic terms. As a result, they do not understand what an effective tool of social control such a culture provides and how it prevents the development of crime and other social deviations, whose incidence is increasing dramatically in industrial societies to the point of rendering them almost ungovernable.

Only now is this, the most important and the least understood of all sociological principles, coming to be generally appreciated. In Benin it is coming to be sensed by an increasing number of people, among whom there is growing reaction against the alien western way of life and, at the same time, renewed interest in their traditional culture.

First printed in *The Ecologist* Vol. 6, No. 6, July 1976.

# Learning

In line with empiricist theory, the tendency has been to explain behaviour in terms of the influence of the environment, i.e. as responses dictated by external stimuli, and there has been a corresponding neglect of the influence of the inherited set of instructions or innate releasing mechanisms (I.R.M.), as Lorenz calls them, that must determine the generalities of a behaviour pattern.

An organism is not born with a blank mind — the *tabula rasa* of the empiricists — but with a general set of instructions and a corresponding general model reflecting its evolutionary experience, which will slowly be differentiated so as to adapt them to the requirements of its specific environment.

This fact is apparent from a number of experiments on different types of animals. Fantz[151] experimented on a sample of 1,000 chicks. He found that they pecked 100 times more often at sphere-shaped objects than at pyramidical-shaped ones. The chicks were hatched in darkness and tested on their first exposure to light, from which it must follow that this behaviour can only be explained on the basis of innate tendencies. Tinbergen[23] found that newly-hatched herring gulls preferred pecking at objects which resembled the bill of the parent from which they were fed. Marked preferences for certain specific objects were also established among baby chimps. Fantz conducted similar experiments with children. In one of these, 49 children, aged from 4 days to 6 months, were presented with:

> ". . . three flat objects, the size and shape of a head. On one we painted a stylized face in black on a pink background, on the second we re-arranged the features in a scrambled pattern, and on the third we painted a solid patch of black at one end, with an area equal to that covered by the features . . . The results were about the same for all age levels: the infants looked most often at the real face, looked slightly less often at the scrambled face, and largely ignored the control pattern."[151]

From such experiments, Fantz concludes:

"Lowly chicks as well a lofty primates perceive and respond to form without experience if given the opportunity at the appropriate age of development. Innate knowledge of the environment is demonstrated by the preference of newly-hatched chicks for forms likely to be edible and by the interest of young infants in kinds of form that will later aid in object recognition, social responsiveness and spatial orientation. This primitive knowledge provides a foundation for the vast accumulation of knowledge through experience."

The modifications brought about to this general model are normally referred to as 'learning'. Its role is not to alter innate behavioural tendencies so much as to enable them to be satisfied with ever-greater precision.

Thus an embryo will develop not merely because its environmental conditions are correct, but also because it contains a complex set of general instructions, that, as a result of interaction with its environment, will be slowly differentiated.

One of the consequences of adopting this model of behaviour is that the notion of learning by trial and error is no longer tenable. Thus, if we put a rat into a maze, we know that it can be taught to find its way out. However, before hitting upon the correct route, it will have to make a series of unsuccessful trials. Now, would it be possible to put order into this series, or must each trial be considered merely a random one? The trial-and-error theory appears to favour the latter hypothesis. However, it can be shown that random behaviour is not a scientific concept. Where there is order, there must be instructions, and a corresponding organisation of information, i.e. a model.

Looked at slightly differently, if the rat is supposed to find its way through the maze, what will determine its first trial? If a hundred possible moves are open to it, why should it start off by making one rather than any other? If the move it makes is haphazard, why should not all the others be haphazard, too? Is a rat behaving in a haphazard way when it chooses to eat a piece of cheese rather than an iron nail, or when it feeds its family rather than that of some other rat? If not, which actions are to be considered haphazard and which are not? The answer is that *the notion of non-directive haphazard trial-and-error learning is irreconcilable with our basic knowledge of behaviour. Instead, one must regard each action as based on what, in the light of a systemic model, constitutes the most probable hypothesis.* This hypothesis will have a higher probability of being correct, i.e. of leading to adaptive behaviour, the greater is the organisation of the model on which it is based. Thus it will be higher in the case of the action undertaken by a man than in that undertaken by a rat, which in turn will be higher than that undertaken by an earthworm. Nevertheless, all the actions of the man, the rat and the earthworm, as Craik [13] was the first to show, must be regarded as based on hypotheses as to the nature of their environment, or rather, *of their relationship with their environment.* Supposing that the first move made by the rat, rather than lead it towards an opening, on the contrary led it to a further cul-de-sac, the model responsible for this error would have to be modified. Thus, when the rat made its next move, the environmental situation would be interpreted in the light of a new model — one that had taken into account the failure of its predecessor to interpret correctly the short-term environmental situation in which the rat had found itself, and one furnishing an ever-more precise representation of the system for the purpose of finding its way out of the maze. In other words, each action could be regarded as a correction of an error, and if we regarded these actions as forming a series, the latter would be 'damped', in the sense that the errors were being progressively reduced, i.e. the system would be tending towards ever-greater stability.

# The Empiricist Fallacy

The empiricist thesis is demonstrably false and that empiricism, or its modern version, logical positivism, should still be taught as gospel in our universities is truly scandalous.

A few considerations should suffice to demonstrate its falsehood. The first is that a child's mind at birth is far from being the *tabula rasa* which empiricism implies. A child at birth must be in possession of a rudimentary knowledge of the nature of its environment reflecting the experience of its species (see Appendix VII) which would not otherwise display stability or continuity. The fact is that a system's behaviour must be based on information that *itself displays continuity*. Each generation must inherit information which reflects the experience of its ancestors going back into the mists of time. As already pointed out, that is why genetic information is so stable. If it were more plastic and could permit adaptations to changes based on the experience of one or two generations only, it might give rise to adaptations to freak conditions unlikely ever to recur. The species involved would be unstable and hence could not survive.

There is yet another reason why the empiricist thesis must be false. Building up information means improving the model so that it may serve as a basis for ever more adaptive behaviour, and this improvement, contrary to what empiricists may think, does not simply consist in accumulating more data but in organising it. The establishment of a new relationship between two of the variables of a model (thinking, in other words), permitting an improved explanation of certain observable data, must increase the information contained within the model without involving the simultaneous detection of data. In this sense the 'rationalist thesis' which empiricists, over the last two hundred years, have been at pains to discredit must be regarded as correct.

Needless to say scientists have sought to overcome this limitation imposed on their ability to understand things by strict adherence to the empiricist thesis. Physicists have introduced into their model variables which correspond to nothing that can be perceived by us even with the aid of the electron microscope. Though they may insist these are hypothetical

123

until such time as their presence can be demonstrated empirically, they treat them, in effect, as if their presence had been substantiated. This is not the case, however, in other disciplines where many of the factors that are relevant to explaining any given situation are ignored because they cannot be perceived.

Finally, the empiricist notion that a hypothesis becomes a fact once it is verified empirically would be true if perception were the objective measuring rod which empiricists take it to be. Since, as we have seen, perception simply involves formulating a hypothesis, to verify a hypothesis empirically simply means to see if it is compatible with another hypothesis.

The fact is that in certain conditions, people will often refuse to accept empirical evidence that conflicts with their basic values, or, more precisely, with the generalities of their cultural pattern.

In the case of such a conflict, the observed facts tend to be modified to fit the general model rather than the reverse. Thus most primitive tribes leading a sedentary agricultural life have their rainmakers. The efficacy of the magical rites performed to induce rain is doubted by nobody. Such a belief survives unscathed, because failure to produce rain will not be attributed to the inefficacy of the rituals, *but to some technical failure in their performance*, such as the presence of someone who has violated a taboo.

Similarly, in all the so-called higher religions, there is a general belief in the efficacy of prayer as a means of acquiring the intervention in worldly matters of some supernatural being. The fact that in no single instance is evidence available to point to such an intervention does not in any way detract from the belief in its efficacy.

Even more illustrative is the behaviour of the Jivaro Indians of Eastern Ecuador. Harner[152] describes how they believe that a man possesses a number of different souls. Apart from the true soul, or 'nekaswakan', he can at times also possess another type of soul, called a 'muisak', or avenging soul. But he also acquires an 'aroutam' soul, which is the one they treasure the most, and whose acquisition as the result of a complex ritual confers upon them invulnerability in war. This soul, after another ritual, leaves the body of its host. However, its power remains, ebbing away only very slowly. It is at this point that the Jivaro, who have just acquired and lost an aroutam soul, must join a killing party whose role it is to kill a member of some other tribe. This is an essential part of aroutam ritual, as it is only by repeated killings that one can replace the ebbing soul with a new one.

Though they are supposed to have complete invulnerability, it occasionally occurs that the killing party is unsuccessful, and one of their members is killed in the attack. When this happens, the Jivaro are not led to revise their belief in the invulnerability conferred by the aroutam soul. On the contrary, the other members of the expedition ". . . simply consider the death to be evidence that the deceased had already lost his aroutam soul without realising it."

On the other hand, the Jivaro are consistent enough in their belief to 'realise' that their killing expedition would have little success if their intended victim were protected by an aroutam soul. "A man who has killed repeatedly, called 'Kakaram', or 'powerful one', is rarely attacked because his enemies feel that the protection provided by him by his constantly replaced souls would make any assassination attempt against him fruitless." So they await the signs of weakness on the part of the intended victim, or ". . . the first-hand observation that the enemy was lacking in forcefulness of speech" which is considered to provide important evidence that the aroutam soul's power has left the intended victim. In any case, he is only attacked if the raiders believe that he has lost his aroutam soul. If they should fail to kill him, this would not cast any doubt as to the vulnerability of people who have been abandoned by their aroutam souls. On the contrary, failure would be attributed to the fact that ". . . the enemy still retained the soul, or had a second one in reserve."

There is a tendency to laugh at such tales, of which innumerable examples can be found among tribal peoples. However, as has been shown in this book, we behave in precisely the same way. Empirical verification, in fact, is only effective, when the verifier has no psychological stake in the outcome.

# How Hypotheses are formed

Models or hypotheses are postulated. However, this does not convey very much information on the actual process involved; no more, in fact, than to say that they are simply reached by 'intuition'.

Postulation cannot just occur at random. Some mechanism must be involved, and it must be possible to determine and formulate the principles underlying it.

The obvious question to ask is what must be the relationship of the hypothesis postulated to all other hypotheses that might be postulated? The equally obvious answer is that it must have the highest probability in terms of the system's model. Thus, if a bridge-player is to maximise his chances of winning over a period, his model must provide him with the most probable distribution of the cards yet to be played among the three other players. Similar probability calculations are required on the part of all gamblers if they are to maximise their chances of success. A little reflection will reveal that this must apply to all behavioural processes. In each case, *the hypothesis that is postulated in order to give rise to adaptive responses must be the one that has the highest probability*. The fact that this is not evident at first sight, as it is in a game of chance, is probably because what constitutes the most probable hypothesis to explain a situation will be different in the case of each different act, since the model in terms of which probabilities must be calculated will, like Heraclitus's river, be modified with each experience.

Are we not over-estimating the capacity of simple organisms in suggesting that they are capable of making such precise calculations? I do not think so. The ability of certain organisms to perform mathematical feats which would test the capacity of the most able mathematician has been clearly demonstrated.

Experiments with the lesser white-throated warbler have revealed that they are guided by the stars during their migrations. The skill with which they are able to do this is quite surprising. Sauer writes: [153]

"Warblers have a remarkable hereditary mechanism for orientating themselves by the stars, a detailed image of the starry configuration in the sky, coupled with a precise time sense which relates the heavenly canopy to the geography of the earth at every time and season. At their very first glimpse of the sky, the birds automatically know the right direction. Without the benefit of previous experience, with no key except the stars, the birds are able to locate themselves in time and space, and to find their way to their destined post."

Not only does this 'time-sense' allow them to take account of the sun's motion across the sky, but it must also be "able to make adjustments to astronomical evolution, for, in the course of time, the pattern of conservation in the sky is slowly but constantly changing".

It is clear that these birds are in possession of an advanced piece of measuring equipment, which our best engineers would have difficulty in designing.

The Nile fish *gymnarcus niloticus* darts among rocks in muddy water after the small fish on which it feeds, and never bumps into anything, in spite of the fact that its eyes are quite degenerate and only sensitive to extremely bright light. Lissmann, [154] who spent twelve years experimenting with this fish, found that it owed its capacity for finding its way around so skillfully to its ability to discriminate between minute differences in the conductivity of the objects in its immediate environment. This skill was so developed that it could tell the difference between mixtures of different proportions of tap water and distilled water entirely on the basis of their different conductivity. If salts or acids were added to the distilled water so that its electrical conductivity matched that of the tap water, it could no longer discriminate between them. Here again, a complicated calculation must be made. To give an idea of the precision involved, Lissmann[154] worked out:

". . . that *Gymnarcus* can respond to a continuous direct-current electric stimulus of about .15 microvolt per centimeter, a value that agrees reasonably well with the calculated sensitivity required to recognize a glass rod two millimeters in diameter. This means that an individual sense organ should be able to convey information about a current change as small as .003 micromicroampere. Extended over the integration time of 25 milliseconds, this tiny current corresponds to a movement of some 1,000 univalent, or singly charged, ions."

Similarly, Noel Martin [93] notes the extraordinary mathematical ability of spiders:

"Spiders act as if they had the brain of first-class mathematicians. For them, space has properties which make its structure quite unique. Moreover, these properties are dynamic. Each time a spider spins a web, it must cope with changing conditions, for the construction of a web involves such variable factors as wind direction, weather protection, exposure to sunlight, and the abundance of prey. The web itself is a masterpiece of construction. It has all the ideal properties which engineers look for — maximum resistance and maximum efficiency, combined with minimum use of material.

". . . The bee is another insect which seems to have great mathematical gifts. Honeycombs are built according to maximum efficiency principles. Being hexagonal, the cells make use of available space in the most economic and symmetrical way possible, and the angle between adjoining cells is such that the smallest possible amount of wax is required for their construction."

Even more illustrative of an organism's capacity to calculate probabilities on the basis of its model of the system is the behaviour of the didiera in Madagascar and the baobob trees in Africa, which are capable of filling the cells of their trunks with water during the rainy season. Many other plants, such as cacti, can do the same thing. Certain of these are capable of storing water in their cells over long periods. The more water they store in their cells, the slower is their metabolism, which can almost come to a halt if they are saturated. On the other hand, the more water they can store, the greater is the period they can last without rain. In order to be able to store up the optimum amount of water in their cells, which must correspond to the minimum amount which they require to see them through a drought, they have perfected a method of forecasting the amount of rain that there will be in the succeeding months. Researchers from The Massachussetts Institute of Technology have studied such cacti in the Mohave desert in South California for four years. They discovered that if after rainfall the cacti filled their cells to one-third or one-half of their capacity, it would invariably rain during the next two or three months. On one occasion they found that the plants had filled their cells to full capacity. It did not rain at all for the next 685 days. It is evident that to maximise their chance of survival, the amount of water they must store is the minimum necessary for their requirements. This can only be calculated by predicting with the maximum degree of probability what the rainfall is likely to be in the following months, a calculation which they appear to perform with astonishing precision.

Again, it may be thought that these examples are simply curiosities of nature. On the contrary, if our thesis is correct, they are but striking examples of a principle in terms of which must be regarded perception and thought processes at all levels of complexity.

Thus, when I look out of my window and see a tree, a road, and people walking to and fro, I am in fact formulating a hypothesis as to the nature of the environmental data isolated by my detecting mechanisms that has the highest probability in the light of my systemic model. The same is true when I identify one of the passers-by as John Smith, and also when I assume that he is going home for dinner. And so it is when I guess that his dinner will consist of shepherd's pie and bananas and custard.

In each case, I am formulating that hypothesis which, in the light of my model of the environment, has the highest probability, even though there may be a reduction in the degree of probability involved as we proceed from the first case to the last.

# Subjectivity of Perception

If perception were a purely 'mechanical' process, environmental data would provide one with a very different image of the environment from that which we in fact 'perceive'. This tends to confirm that it is achieved by the 'brain' or neuro-cybernism, i.e. a 'hypothesis' based on our particular mental model of our relationship with our environment.

For instance, we can differentiate between movements in our environment and shifts of the image on the retina due to the movement of our own eyes. We are capable of perceiving 'phantom colours', such as white and purple, which constitute gaps in the spectrum. We can distinguish between extreme cold and extreme heat, both of which transmit identical messages to the brain. Babies see everything the right way up, whereas, if they were to depend on their detecting mechanisms, they would see everything upside down. In general, as Kohler [155] writes:

". . . the image is 'better' than it should be, considering the known defects in the visual system. For example, the lens of the eye is not corrected for spherical aberration; hence straight lines should look slightly curved. By the same token, lines of a certain curvature should appear straight. It is well known that the eye is not corrected for colour; as a result, different wavelengths of light — originating at a common point — do not come to a focus on the retina. One would expect this defect, called chromatic aberration, to have a noticeable effect on vision, but it does not, except under special conditions."

Equally inexplicable, in terms of a 'mechanical' theory of perception, is the phenomenon of 'constancy', whereby things continue to look the same to us in spite of the fact that they have been physically modified. For instance, particular objects remain the same colour in spite of the fact that they may be subjected to different lights. Konrad Lorenz [156] writes:

"I see the top of my desk in always the same light brown colour, regardless of whether I look at it in the bluish morning light, in the strongly reddish light of the later afternoon, or in the yellow lights of an electric bulb. Factually the top of my desk reflects very different wavelengths under each one of these different circumstances, but my perception reports little or nothing of this. What it reports to me is, in the last analysis, no colour at all but a *property* constantly attached to the object, the property of reflecting light of one type of wavelength better than that of another . . .''

Lorenz [156] explains this in the following way:

"All apparati of constancy . . . are 'ratiomorphic', in the strictest sense, for all contain processes analagous to induction and deduction, all contain 'hypotheses' whose attunement is not absolute, but only to a high degree probable.''

Warren J. Wittreich [157] sees it in much the same way:

"When we watch a person walk away from us, his image shrinks in size. But since we know for a fact that he is not shrinking, we make an unconscious correction, and 'see' him as retaining his full stature. Past experience tells us what his true stature is with respect to our own. Any sane and dependable expectation of the future requires that he have the same true stature when we next encounter him. *Our perception is thus a prediction; it embraces the past and the future as well as the present.*"

## The influence of expectation and anxiety on perception

Numerous experiments have demonstrated that people do not in fact see what is revealed by detecting devices, but rather what they *expect* to see — which will vary in each case in accordance with experience and hence with the personality of the perceiver. This only appears explicable in terms of a cybernismic theory of perception. For instance, Ittleson and Kilpatrick [158] have shown that:

"If a subject sits in a dark room, in which he can only see two star points of light, both equidistant from the observer, one of which is brighter, when the subject closes one eye, and keeps his head still, the brighter point of light looks nearer than the dimmer one. Such apparent differences are due not only to brightness but also to direction from the observer. If two points of light of equal brightness are situated near the floor, one about a foot above the other, the upper one will generally be perceived as farther away than the lower one; if they are near the ceiling the lower one will appear farther away.''

This they explain in the following way:

"When presented with two star points of different brightness, a person unconsciously 'bets' or 'assumes' that the two points, being similar, are probably identical (i.e. of equal brightness), and therefore that the one that seems brighter must be nearer. Similarly, the observed facts in the case of two star points placed vertically one above the other suggests that *when we look down we assume, on the basis of past experience, that objects in the lower part of the visual field are nearer than the objects in the upper part; when we look up, we assume that the opposite is true.*

"These phenomena cannot be explained by referring to 'reality' because 'reality' and perception do not correspond. They cannot be explained by reference to the pattern in the retina of the eye, because, for any given retinal pattern, there are an infinite number of brightness-size-distance combinations to which that pattern might be related. *When faced with such a situation, in which an unlimited number of possibilities can be related to a given retinal pattern, the organism apparently calls upon its previous experience and assumes that what has been most probable in the past is most probable in the immediate occasion.*"

The cybernismic nature of perception is illustrated even more dramatically by experiments in which the subject

". . . wears a pair of glasses fitted with so-called anisiekonic lenses, which are ground in such a way that they give images of different sizes and shape to the two retinas. This produces very marked distortions of any object which the subject visualizes mainly through the use of two-eyed stereoscopic vision."

In this way, the distortion produced by our normal detecting apparati is increased. In these experiments the subject succeeds in correcting the induced distortions, and actually sees what he expects to see, i.e. what in the light of his experience, *or rather in the light of the model of the system that he has built up as a result of his experience, is judged to be the most probable interpretation of the environmental signals.*

Other experiments have been conducted in a distorted room as originally designed by Adelbert Ames Jr. at the Institute for Associated Research, Hanover, N.H.:

". . . in which the floor slopes up to the right of the observer, the real wall recedes from right to left, and the windows are of different sizes and trapezoidal in shape. When an observer looks at this room with one eye from a certain point, the room appears completely normal, as if the floor were level, the real wall at right angles to the line of sight and the windows rectangular and of the same size. Presumably the observer chooses this particular appearance instead of some other because of the assumptions he brings to the occasion. If he now takes a long stick and tries to touch the various parts of the room, he will be unsuccessful, even though he has gone into the situation knowing the true shape of the room. With practice, however, he becomes more and more success-ful in touching what he wants to touch with the stick. More important, he sees the room more and more in its true shape even though the stimulus pattern on his retina has remained unchanged.''

In the typical experiments carried out in the Ames room, the viewer sees a normal shaped room and instead sees distortion in the appearance of the people in the room; thus:

''A viewer observing the faces of her husband and another man at the windows of the small room reported that her husband's face remained unchanged, though she observed the expected distortion in the face of the other man. Similarly, the other man appeared to grow or shrink as he walked to and fro in the larger room, while her husband underwent no change in size whatsoever. Cantril called this reaction the 'honi' phenomenon, after the woman's nickname.''

Wittreich [157] and others made further experiments to explain this phenomenon. It was found that though other married couples did not always behave in this way, they did if the husband was an authority figure, and the wife felt a certain anxiety when she saw him. Soldiers were found to behave in this way with regard to their senior officers, as were amputees when they saw other amputees.

The results of these experiments are in keeping with the cybernismic theory of perception. Wittreich [157] concludes:

*''Though I have spoken here of reacting to people and perceiving them as two distinct processes, these processes should not be regarded as being so separable as this wording suggests. In using such terms we are simply abstracting two aspects of a single process. The evidence points to the fusion of feeling and perceiving in a deeper understanding of the process of living.''*

Ittleson and Kilpatrick interpret the results of such experiments thus:

*''All these experiments, and many more that have been made, suggest strongly that perception is never a sure thing, never an absolute revela-tion of 'what is'. Rather, what we see is a prediction — our own personal construction designed to give us the best possible bet for carrying out our purposes in action.''*

### The influences of ontogenetic development on perception
If perception is the interpretation of data in terms of a model, then the value of the interpretation will depend on the quality of the model, which in turn will be a function of the number and value of the variables in terms of which the data can be classified and their degree of organisation.

This will increase during phylogeny and ontogeny. Thus the information derived from perception must be higher in the case of man than in that of an amoeba, in the case of an adult than in that of a child, and in the case of a knowledgeable man than in that of an ignorant one.

Bowen[159] shows that a child's view of the world is rudimentary, and that it slowly develops as he grows up. The adult will have a totally different view, corresponding to his more highly developed cerebral cortex and to the considerable knowledge he will undoubtedly have accumulated over the years. This implies that what one sees is determined by one's upbringing and education, a thesis that is confirmed by a number of experiments designed to determine the effect on perception of being deprived of the ability to perceive normal environmental data for long periods. Melzack[160] tells of such experiments:

"We raised Scottish Terriers in isolation from infancy to maturity so that they were deprived of normal environmental stimuli, including the bodily knocks and scrapes that young animals get in the course of growing up. We were surprised to find that when these dogs grew up they failed to respond normally to a flaming match. Some of them repeatedly poked their nose into the flame and sniffed at it as long as it was present. If they snuffed it out, they reacted similarly to a second flaming match and even to a third. Others did not sniff at the match but made no effort to get away when we touched their noses with the flame repeatedly. These dogs also endured pinpricks with little or no evident pain. In contrast, litter mates that had been reared in a normal environment recognized potential harm so quickly that we were usually unable to touch them with the flame or pin more than once.

"This astonishing behaviour of dogs reared in isolation cannot be attributed to a general failure of the sensory conducting systems. Intense electric shock elicited violent excitement. Moreover, reflex movements made by the dogs during contact with fire and pinprick indicate that they may have felt something during stimulation, but the lack of any observable emotional disturbance, apart from the reflex movements, suggests that their perception of actual damage to the skin was highly abnormal."

Equally illustrative are the cases described by Riesen[161] of patients operated on for congenital cataracts:

"These patients, who have passed all their lives in near-blindness, ranging from the bare ability to tell day from night to some ability to distinguish colours and localize light, invariably report an immediate awareness of change after a successful operation. They begin at once to distinguish differences in the parts of the visual field, although they cannot identify any object or describe its shape. After a few days' practice they can name colours. From this point on progress is slow, often highly discouraging, and some patients never get beyond the ability to distinguish brightness and colour. Others, over a period of months and even years, develop the ability to identify simple geometric figures, read letters and numbers and, in rare cases, to identify faces. During their efforts to improve their visual skill, the patients go through a long period of picking out elements in an object and inferring the nature of the object from these elements, often erroneously. For example, a child of twelve, some months after her operation, is reported by her doctor to have pointed to a picture and called it 'a camel', 'because it has a hump'. What she identified as a hump was the dorsal fin of a fish.''

The effect of isolation on perception does not differ in any way from its effect on other cybernismic functions.

A child isolated from its normal social and physical environment for a long period will, once restored to it, be capable of but the most rudimentary behaviour. This is illustrated by the recorded instances of children found in a wild state, or brought up by animals. In none of these cases was the child ever capable of learning more than a few words of human language, for instance, in spite of a considerable effort on the part of their tutors. This is particularly true in the cases of Victor de l'Aveyron, Kamala of Midnapore, Dina Sanichar and Anna of Pennsylvania. They remained mentally stunted in every respect. Dina Sanichar, for instance, who died at the age of forty, probably never achieved the mental age of one and a half; and Kamala, who lived to be seventeen, that of three and half. [162]

Numerous experiments with monkeys lead one to the same conclusion. According to Harlow and Kuenne, [163] they all

". . . indicate that animals, human and subhuman, must learn to think. Thinking does not develop spontaneously as an expression of innate abilities; it is the end result of a long learning process. Years ago, the British biologist, Thomas Henry Huxley, suggested that the 'brain secretes thought as the liver secretes bile'. Nothing could be further from the truth. The brain is essential to thought, but the untutored brain is not enough, no matter how good a brain it may be.''

These experiments all tend to confirm the thesis that perception involves the postulation of hypotheses in the light of a model. At birth, when this model is rudimentary, the hypotheses based on it will be correspondingly so, and, as the model evolves, so will there be an improvement in perception and cybernization in general, permitting thereby a corresponding increase in behavioural stability.

**The influence of suggestion on perception**
The fact that the sensations and perceptions of hypnotised people can be affected very radically by the hypnotist is well-known. Bernheim was apparently the first to propose that hypnosis is in fact nothing more than an extreme form of 'suggestion'. Since then it has become apparent that everybody is continually being subjected to various forms of suggestion that will influence them to a greater or lesser degree, in accordance with their particular degree of suggestibility, and also in accordance with the prestige of the source of the suggestion. A large number of experiments have been conducted to determine the effect of suggestion and hence of public opinion on people's perceptions. The result of these experiments has been to show that perception is very much open to the influence of public opinion. To quote Asch: [164]

"When confronted with opinions contrary to their own, many subjects apparently shifted their judgement in the direction of the view of the majorities or the experts.
"The late psychologist Edward L. Thorndyke reported that he had succeeded in modifying the aesthetic preferences of adults by this procedure. Other psychologists reported that people's evaluations of the merit of a literary passage could be raised or lowered by ascribing the passage to different authors. Apparently the sheer weight of numbers or authority sufficed to change opinions, even when no arguments for the opinions themselves were provided."

In a series of experiments conducted by Asch[164] and others, a group of students at Harvard were presented with lines of different sizes, and were told to graduate them according to size. All the members of the group except one, chosen at random, had been previously instructed to give the sizes in the wrong order. The odd man out was thus faced with a dilemma: he must either give preference to the evidence of his 'senses', or to that of the opinion of the majority. How did he react? This experiment was carried out 123 times, with different groups, and in each case a different person was put in the minority position. In 36.8% of these experiments, the latter yielded to the opinion of the majority. Asch shows that people can be classified in accordance with their tendency to do so. Behaviour in this respect is highly consistent:

"Those who strike out on the path of independence do not, as a rule, succumb to the majority even over an extended series of trials, while those who choose the path of compliance are unable to free themselves as the ordeal is prolonged."

Asch shows considerable concern at the implications of these experiments. Thus:

"That we have found the tendency to conformity in our society so strong that reasonably intelligent and well-meaning young people are willing to call white black is a matter of concern. It raises questions about our ways of education and about the values that guide our conduct."

This behaviour is totally in keeping with the cybernismic view of perception. The model that a person builds up of his environment must be very much influenced by those of his fellow citizens. If it were not, then different societies could not develop different cultural patterns.

The implication of this is enormous. It explains, among other things, how scientists who have been imbued with the values of industrial civilisation will generally interpret data in such a way as to rationalise conclusions that are consistent with these values. Only the strongest and most independent among them will be able to come to conclusions that are inconsistent with these values.

*No fact could be more indicative of the total inadequacy of perception for obtaining information or for verifying hypotheses with that measure of objectivity that is required of science.*

# Subjective Classifications in Science

Processes occurring at a relatively low level of complexity, i.e. at the atomic, molecular, or cellular stage, lie to a large extent outside our immediate experience, and are therefore less subject to subjective thinking. However, as soon as we leave this level, and especially when we attain that of the human being, and the societies into which he is organized, we gradually find ourselves heir to a plethora of subjective concepts, in terms of which we have been taught to think since childhood. Examples are mind, consciousness, memory, religion, democracy, etc. Even when we admit the desirability, for scientific purposes, of adopting objective classifications, we are loath to abandon such subjective terms, which are so well established in the society we live in and so firmly ingrained in our minds that we tend to regard them, unconsciously at least, as real constituents of the environment. Rather than be forced to admit that we are guilty of subjectivity and nominal realism, there is a tendency to avoid defining such terms altogether. In some cases, we even persuade ourselves that a definition is not required. Such terms as 'life', and 'culture', for instance, have never, to my knowledge, been adequately defined. This, however, has not prevented innumerable academics from devoting their lives to the study of these subjects, and accumulating vast amounts of 'empirical data' that appear to be relevant. As Woodger writes:

"Nothing is more striking in this science than the contrast between the brilliant skill, ingenuity and care bestowed upon observation and experiment, and the almost complete neglect of caution in regard to the definition and use of the concepts in terms of which its results are expressed."[165]

Let us take the term 'life.' George Wald, a Nobel prizewinning biologist, observes the fact that no one has in fact defined it. Thus I quote:

"A curious thing about biology is that it flourishes as a science of life without attempting to define life. We are often told that the beginning step in any science is to define its terms, indeed, to give them operational definitions, by which one usually means to describe the operations by which they can be measured.

"Biologists long ago became convinced that it is not useful to define life. The trouble with any such definition is that one can always construct a model that satisfies the definition, yet clearly it is not alive . . . And, of course, we do not measure life. We can measure many of its manifestations accurately; and we combine those with others that we observe, but perhaps cannot measure, to make up our concept of what it means to be alive. The life itself is neither observed nor measured. It is a summary of and judgement upon our measurements and observations. What biologists do about life is to recognize it . . ."[166]

Contrary to Wald, I maintain that all precise terms must be definable if they are to be used for the purposes of building an effective model.

When I say 'definable', I am referring to an objective definition, or the role that a variable plays in a given model.

The term 'life' is applicable to systems at a particular level of complexity, usually associated with the development of a cell, though this is by no means a clear delimitation, since precellular systems such as bacteria are considered to fall within the field of biology.

The discovery of the virus caused a shift in the exact field of biology, since these 'independent genes', having a still simpler organisation than the bacteria, manifest certain characteristics of living things when in a vegetative stage, though when deprived of a source of protein they will revert to a crystalline stage, at which point they appear to be little more than crystallised nucleic acids.

Naturally, it has not yet been decided whether viruses fall within the field of biology or not, as no one can decide to what extent they are in fact alive.

*My contention is that such systems cannot be classified as living or non-living things because 'life' has not been defined, and no satisfactory definition of 'life' is available because it does not constitute a scientific classification.*

Rather than refer to the role played by a particular process in a larger one, or a particular situation in a larger one, as is the case with the classification 'level of complexity', for instance, the classification 'life' corresponds rather to the way things appear to us. *It is a subjective classification rather than an objective one.*

George Wald's article provides us with another example of the same principle. I quote:

"Once, years ago, I was asked to attend a conference entitled 'Fatigue in the reading of microfilm.' For the first two days, we all gave papers; they were about everything to do with vision except fatigue. A round-table conference on the third day was opened with a paper on fatigue. He began by defining fatigue as a deterioration in performance. He then described giving experimental subjects a battery of about a dozen different tests of performance, then keeping them awake for two or three days and re-testing them. None showed any demonstrable deterioration in performance. The psychologists kept assuring us that nevertheless he was certain that these persons were fatigued.

"I learned then that this familiar concept, fatigue, cannot be adequately defined. The most rigorous operation for determining fatigue seems to be to ask a person whether he feels tired. For a long period there was a Fatigue Laboratory in operation at Harvard University. At one time its Director, reviewing the subject of industrial fatigue, concluded that it is largely boredom. And how does one define boredom?"[166]

The trouble with this treatment of the term 'fatigue' is that it is being used in two different senses. To define fatigue as 'diminished ability' appears to be a legitimate scientific definition that can be measured. Personally, I should prefer a slightly narrower definition in terms of diminishing ability, due to over-use of a particular faculty. Thus a curve could be drawn for most of our behavioural mechanisms, showing that up to a certain point the more they are made use of, the more highly they will develop. A point, however, will be reached when 'fatigue sets in'. At this point, the mechanism is being used beyond its normal possibilities, and performance, which until now has slowly increased with use, will begin to deteriorate. *The only argument that Wald could furnish against the use of such a term as 'fatigue' was that people showing such diminished ability did not actually 'feel fatigued', i.e. the objective use of the term did not correspond to its subjective use.*

It must be clear that two different concepts are involved. The first is of definite scientific value; the second, the subjective one, is not. What a man says he feels, any psychologist will tell us, is not a reliable guide to his physical state. The man could have been subjected to various forms of suggestion, or out of sheer vanity he may not wish to admit that he was not in the pink of health. Fatigue used in this subjective sense can conceivably have a place in a psychological model in which people's sensations, or more precisely, people's statements about their sensations, are taken as a guide to their physical condition; but not in an objective model, in which 'diminished ability' will be translatable in terms of lower efficiency. *Indeed, whenever a currently-used term appears difficult to define, it is well worth considering the possibility that it does not constitute an objective classification, but merely a subjective one.*

# The Objectivisation of
# Scientific Information

It cannot be denied that those scientific disciplines dealing with the simplest type of behaviour, in particular physics, have been extremely successful. However, as physics has developed, it has become ever less dependent on perception for the purposes of building up scientific knowledge. In fact, as physics has developed, so has man's view of the physical world become couched in ever less subjective terms, i.e. terms which are ever less those of our own personal experience. As Konrad Lorenz says, "Every step of knowledge in physics means 'taking off a pair of glasses.'[156]

Von Bertalanffy writes: "It is an essential characteristic of science that it progressively de-anthropomorphises, that it progressively eliminates those traits which are due to specifically human experiences. Physics necessarily starts with the sensory experience of the eye, the ear, the thermal sense, etc., and thus builds up fields like optics, acoustics, the theory of heat, which correspond to the realms of sensory experience. Soon, however, these fields fuse into such that do not have any more relation to the 'visualisable' or 'intuitable': optics and electricity fuse into electro-magnetic theory; mechanics and the theory of heat into statistical thermodynamics, etc."[98]

Thus a satisfactory science of thermodynamics could not have developed so long as heat was merely equated with the sensation it produced in us. Such an identification must be made if we are to adopt the strict empiricist thesis. In this sphere, as in many others, empiricism could have provided a barrier to any further development of knowledge. Such a standpoint was abandoned in favour of the not altogether unreasonable hypothesis that if something produced heat there must be a reason for it, and that the sensation called heat that we felt was but the way in which this thing was affecting us. *The thing, in fact, could be studied apart from the sensation it produced in us.* Heat was found to be a kind of energy that could be exploited. It was analysed in terms of the movement of particles and various temperature scales were developed. Slowly, the theory of thermodynamics came into being.

Indeed, as science advances, the variables used are further and further divorced from those of our experience. Thus the physicist's concept of 'time' as dependent on velocity and as inseparable from space; the pi-meson with its lifespan of two millionths of a second; the electron that weighs only a billionth of a billionth of a billionth of a gram; and anti-particles that may run counter to time and that may originate in the future and become extinct in the past — all of these are obviously totally outside the world of our experience. As Noel-Martin writes:

"Ever since Evariste Galois made his brilliant contribution to mathematics, mathematical thought has explored a world of ideas so far removed from experience as to correspond with no known reality. The great mathematicians of our time can be said to work by intuition rather than by external sense data."[93]

W.H. Thorpe considers that many of the most important theories in the history of science "are arrived at as much by the modes of thought of the artist and of the pure mathematician as by those popularly considered to be characteristic of scientists . . . by great 'leaps of imaginative insight'; leaps which, at the time they were made, may have had very little experimental or observational basis."[122]

Gerald Feinberg shows how this feature of scientific activity was necessary for the understanding of the concept of matter:[167]

"The proper understanding of matter requires the imagination to invent entities not apparent in everyday phenomena. It is the enduring miracle of creative thought that the mind is equal to this task."

Writing of Democritus, he says:

'What is remarkable is that he was willing to make the intellectual leaps of assuming the existence of unobserved objects quite different from those found in ordinary matter, and to account for everyday objects in terms of them. It is in this sense that Democritus is a fore-runner of modern physics, in which the properties of bulk matter are accounted for in terms of atoms and their component particles, which in themselves behave very differently from the way bulk matter does."

Bridgman shows how the modern theory of the atom was developed in this manner:

"This is evidently a construct, because no one ever directly experiences an atom, and *its existence is entirely inferential. The atom was invented to explain constant combining weights in chemistry. For a long time, there was no other experimental evidence of its existence, and it remained a pure invention, without physical reality, useful in discussing a certain group of phenomena.*"[168]

In other fields of study, however, the original subjective vocabulary is still intact. Academics in these fields are busily engaged in the hopeless task of using these subjective variables for the purpose of building up objective knowledge. Can they do otherwise? Man has but a small psychological stake in the behaviour of atoms, at least until such time as he seeks to extract the energy imprisoned within them in power stations and atom bombs. When we pass to the behaviour of people and societies, however, can he really overcome the subjective views with which he has been imbued during the course of his upbringing in his particular cultural group? The answer is undoubtedly no.

# References

1. Edward Hartpole Lecky, 'The political value of history' in *Historical and Political Essays* Longman Green & Co., London, 1908.
2. Henry Thomas Buckle, *A History of Civilization in England* Vol. 11, Grant Richards, London, 1903.
3. Gustave le Bon, *La Psychologie des Foules* Felix Alcan, Paris, 1906.
4. Robert Lowie, *Primitive Society* Routledge and Kegan Paul, London, 1963.
5. Lucy Mair, *Primitive Government* Penguin Books, London, 1962.
6. Fustel de Coulanges, *La Cité Antique* Hachette, Paris, 1927.
7. Maurice Maeterlink, *La Vie des Termites* Paris, 1927.
8. N. Tinbergen, *Social Behaviour in Animals* Methuen, London, 1953. See also: R.W. Gerrard, 'A biologist's view of society' *General Systems Yearbook* Vol. 1, No. 1, 1956.
9. A.D. Hall and R.E. Fagen, 'Definition of system' *General Systems Yearbook* Vol. 1, No. 1, 1956.
10. C.H. Waddington, *The Strategy of the Genes* Allen and Unwin, London, 1957.
11. Richard B. Lee and Erwin Devore (eds.), *Man the Hunter* Aldine, Chicago, 1968.
12. Norman H. Horowitz, 'The gene' *Scientific American* October, 1956.
13. Kenneth Craik, *The Nature of Explanation* Cambridge University Press, Cambridge, 1952.
14. See, for instance, H. Harlow and Margaret K. Harlow, 'A study of animal affection' *Natural History* Vol. LXX, pp. 48-55.
15. Stephen Boyden 'Evolution and Health' *The Ecologist* Vol. 3, No. 8, August, 1973.
16. Alan Moorehead, *The Fatal Impact* Penguin Books, London, 1962.
17. Jay W. Forrester, 'Alternatives to catastrophe' *The Ecologist* Vol. 1, No. 14, September, 1971; Vol. 1, No. 15, October, 1971. See also: Jay W. Forrester, *World Dynamics* Cambridge, Mass., 1971.
18. S. Zuckerman, *The Social Life of Monkeys and Apes* Routledge and Kegan Paul, London, 1932.
19. Sigmund Freud, *Totem and Taboo* Routledge and Kegan Paul, London, 1950.
20. W. Trotter, *The Instinct of the Herd in Peace and War* Fisher Unwin, London, 1916.
21. Bronislaw Malinowski, *Sex and Repression in Savage Society* Routledge and Kegan Paul, London, 1961.
22. George Peter Murdock, *Social Structure* The Free Press, New York, 1965.
23. N. Tinbergen, *The Study of Instinct* The Clarendon Press, Oxford, 1951.
24. Edward Goldsmith, 'Education: what for?' *The Ecologist* Vol. 4, No. 1, January, 1974.
25. George Peter Murdock, 'Changing emphasis in social structure' in *Culture and Society* (G.P. Murdock, ed.) University of Pittsburg Press, Pittsburg, 1965.
26. Melford E. Spiro, 'Is the family universal? The Israeli case' in *A Modern Introduction to the Family* (Norman W. Bell and Ezra F. Vogel, eds.) The Free Press, New York, 1960.
27. E. Kathleen Gough, 'Is the family universal? The Nayar case' in *A Modern Introduction to the Family* (Norman W. Bell and Ezra F. Vogel, eds.) The Free Press, New York, 1960.
28. Erich Fromm, *The Art of Loving* Unwin, London, 1957.
29. A.R. Radcliffe Brown, *Structure and Function in Primitive Society* Cohen and West, London, 1965.
30. Sir Henry Maine, *Ancient Law* London. 1861.
31. Jeannette Mirsky, 'The Eskimos of Greenland' in *Cooperation and Competition among Primitive Peoples* (Margaret Mead, ed.) Beacon Press, Boston, 1961.
32. Ralph Linton, *The Study of Man* Peter Owen, London, 1965.
33. Homer, *The Iliad* 2/362.
34. G. Glotz, *The Greek City* Routledge and Kegan Paul, London, 1950.
35. Amos Rappoport, 'The ecology of housing' *The Ecologist* Vol. 3, No. 1, January, 1973.

36. Claude Levi-Strauss, *Tristes Tropiques* Plon, Paris, 1955.
37. Robert Jaulin, 'Ethnocide' *The Ecologist* Vol. 1, No. 18, December, 1971.
38. Paul Bohannon, 'Africa's Land' *The Centennial Review* Vol. LV, 1960.
39. Raymond Firth, *The Elements of Social Organisation* C.A. Watts & Co., London, 1951.
40. Adolphe Lods, *Israel: From Its Beginnings to the Middle of the Eighth Century* Routledge and Kegan Paul, London, 1932.
41. J.E.S. Thompson, *Mexico before Cortez* New York, 1932.
42. Emile Durkheim, 'The solidarity of occupational groups' in *Theories of Society* (Talcott Parsons, ed.) The Free Press, New York, 1970.
43. J.-P. Waltzing, *Etude Historique sur les Corporations Professionelles chez les Romains* (4 vols.) Memoir of the Royal Academy of Belgium, Charles Peeters, Louvain, 1895-1900.
44. Francis L.K. Hsu, *Under the Ancestor's Shadow* Routledge and Kegan Paul, London, 1949.
45. W. Robertson Smith, *Essays on the Religion of the Semites* Adams and Charles Black, London, 1914.
46. G.E. Von Grunebaum, *Islam: Essays on the Nature and Growth of a Cultural Tradition* Routledge and Kegan Paul, London, 1955.
47. Emile Durkheim and Marcel Mauss, *Primitive Classification* University of Chicago Press, Chicago, 1963.
48. Salomon Reinach, *Orpheus. A History of Religions* Horace Liveright, New York, 1930.
49. Robert Thouless, *An Introduction to the Psychology of Religion* Cambridge University Press, Cambridge, 1971.
50. Sir James Frazer, *The Golden Bough* Macmillan, London, 1923.
51. Julian Huxley, *Religion without Revelation* C.A. Watts & Co., London, 1967.
52. Edward Goldsmith, 'Religion in the light of a general behavioural model' *Systematics* Vol. 8, No. 2, 1970, pp. 91-100.
53. Edward Goldsmith, 'Towards a unified science', a seris of articles in *The Ecologist* Vols. 1-3, 1970-1972.
54. J.S. Furnivall, *Netherlands' India, a Study in Plural Economy* Cambridge University Press, Cambridge, 1939.
55. Lafcadio Hearn, *Japan, an Interpretation* Macmillan, New York, 1904.
56. Edward Tyler, *Primitive Culture* John Murray, London, 1903.
57. E. Driver, *Indians of North America* University of Chicago Press, Chicago, 1961.
58. Cora Dubois, *The People of Alor* Harpers, New York, 1960.
59. W.J. Goode, *Religion among the Primitives* The Free Press, New York, 1964.
60. Hilda Kuper, *The Swazi. A South African Kingdom* Holt, Rinehart, and Winston, New York, 1963.
61. M.J. Herskovits, *Dahomey* Augustin, New York, 1938.
62. Cullen Young, 'The idea of God in Northern Nyasaland' in *African Ideas of God* (Edwin W. Smith, ed.) Edinburgh House Press, London, 1950.
63. Edward Goldsmith, 'The stable society' *The Ecologist* Vol. 1, No. 6, December, 1970.
64. Karl Polanyi, *Primitive, Archaic and Modern Economics* Doubleday, New York, 1968.
65. Quoted by Robert Lowie in *Primitive Society* Routledge and Kegan Paul, London, 1963.
66. J.H. Driberg, 'The secular aspect of ancestor worship in Africa' in *African Ideas of God* (Edwin W. Smith, ed.) Edinburgh House Press, London, 1950.
67. Father Placide Tempels, *Bantu Philosophy* Presence Africaine, Paris, 1948.
68. Paul Schebesta, *Les Pygmées* Gallimard, Paris, 1940.
69. Abraham Kardiner, *The Psychological Frontiers of Society* Columbia University Press, New York, 1945.
70. Homer, *The Odyssey*.
71. Mason Hammond, *City State and World State in Greek and Roman Political Theory until Augustus* Harvard University Press, Cambridge, Mass., 1951.
72. E.A. Wallace Budge, *A History of Egypt. From the End of the Neolithic Period to the Death of Cleopatra, 3 B.C.* (4 vols) London, 1901.
73. Jomo Kenyatta, *Facing Mount Kenya* Secker and Warburg, London, 1953.
74. Edward Hartpole Lecky, *A History of European Morals from Augustus to Charlemagne* Longmans, Green & Co., London, 1905.
75. Stephen Runciman, *The Medieval Manichee* Cambridge University Press, Cambridge, 1947.
76. D.L. Meadows, et al., *Limits to Growth* Potomac Associates, Washington D.C., 1972.
77. Lord Zuckerman, Speech at United Nations Conference on the Human Environment, Stockholm, 1972.
78. Edward Goldsmith, 'The study of cultural behaviour' *The Ecologist* Vol. 3, No. 1, January, 1973.

79. Ross Hume Hall, *Food for Nought* Harper & Row, New York, 1974.
80. Michael and Sheilagh Crawford, *What We Eat Today* Neville Spearman, London, 1972.
81. S.H. Katz and M.V. Young, 'Biosocial Aspects of Breastfeeding' Paper presented at Annual A.A.A.S. Meeting, Boston, 21 February 1976.
82. George Perkins March, *Man and Nature* The Belknap Press of Harvard University Press.
83. J.A. Bierens de Haan, *Animal Psychology* Hutchinson's University Library, London, 1946.
84. Melvin Laird, From a discussion at the First International Conference on the Environmental Future at Helsinki, 1973. See Nicholas Polunin (ed.) *Environmental Future* Macmillan, London, 1973.
85. N. Polunin (ed.) *Environmental Future* Macmillan, London, 1973.
86. Edward Goldsmith, 'Is science a religion?' *The Ecologist*, Vol. 5, No. 2, February 1975.
87. SCEP, *Man's Impact on the Global Environment* MIT Press, Cambridge, Mass., 1971.
88. Charles F. Wurster, 'The effect of pesticides' in *The Environmental Future* (Nicholas Polunin, ed.) Macmillan, London, 1973.
89. *The Ecologist* Vol. 3, No. 9, September 1973, p. 329.
90. Samuel Epstein, *Public Health Hazards from Chemicals in Consumer Products*.
91. D. Saffiotti, quoted by Epstein, ibid.
92. Alvin Weinberg, *Science and Trans-Science*, Minerva 5: 208-222 April 1972, quoted by John E. Blodgett 'Pesticides, Regulation of an evolving technology', in Samuel Epstein and Richard D. Grundy (eds.), *Consumer health and product hazards,* Vol. 2, The MIT Press, Cambridge, Mass., 1974.
93. Charles Noel-Martin, *The Role of Perception in Science* Hutchinson, London, 1963.
94. Quoted by Stuart Chase in *The Tyranny of Words* Methuen, London, 1943.
95. See the *Scientific American* collection *The Frontiers of Perception* W.H. Freeman & Son, London, 1971.
96. Hans Reichenbach, *The Rise of Scientific Philosophy* University Press, California, 1958.
97. James D. Watson, *The Double Helix* Penguin, London, 1973.
98. Ludwig von Bertalanffy, 'General systems theory: a critical review' *General Systems Yearbook* Vol. VII, 1962.
99. Emile Durkheim, *Suicide* Routledge and Kegan Paul, London, 1963.
100. Marvin Opler, 'The Ethnic Difference in Behaviour and Psychopathology: Italian and Irish' *International Journal of Social Psychiatry*, 1956, Vol. II, 11 and 22.
101. K.E. Boulding, 'Economics of the coming spaceship earth' in Henry Jarret (ed.) *Environmental quality in the growing economy* John Hopkins Press, 1966.
102. Nicholas Georgescu Roegen, 'Economics and Entropy' *The Ecologist,* Vol. 2, No. 7, July 1972.
103. Reid Bryson, from an impromptu talk at the Second Environmental Conference at Reykjavik, June 1977.
104. Letitia Obeng, from an impromptu talk at the above Conference.
105. Herman Flohn, from an impromptu talk at the above Conference.
106. Robert Waller, 'The Declining Health of Urban Man' *The Ecologist* Vol. 1, No. 2, August, 1970.
107. Ross Hume Hall, 'Beware of those fabricated foods' *Executive Health* Vol. XII, No. 7, April, 1976.
108. Eric Waddell, 'The Return to Traditional Agricultre' *The Ecologist*, Vol. 7, No. 4, May, 1977.
109. C.C. Hughes and J.M. Hunter, 'Development and Disease in Africa' *The Ecologist* Vol. 2, No. 9, September, 1972.
110. Anatol Rapoport, 'An Essay on Mind' *General Systems Yearbook* Vol. VII, 1962.
111. See Eddison, *The Logic of Modern Physics*, Macmillan, New York, 1961.
112. Norman H. Horowitz, 'The gene' *Scientific American* October, 1956.
113. J.H. Fabre, *Souvenirs Entomoligiques* Series IX, Delagrave, Paris 1879-1909.
114. N. Tinbergen, *Social Behaviour in Animals* Methuen, London, 1953.
115. H.F. Harlow, 'The Evolution of Learning' in *Behavour and Evolution* (A. Roe and G.G. Simpson eds.) Yale University Press, 1964.
116. W.E.H. Stanner, 'Dreaming, an Australian World View' *Cultural and Social Anthropology* (P.B. Hammond ed.), Macmillan Co., New York, 1964.
117. A.W. Morley, *The Ant World* Penguin Books, London.
118. Caryl P. Haskins, *Of Ants and Men* Prentice Hall, New York, 1939.
119. L. von Bertalanffy, 'The World of Science & The World of Value' *Teachers College Record* Vol. 65, No. 6, March, 1964.
120. J.W.S. Pringle 'On the Parallel betwen Learning and Evolution' *General Systems Yearbook* Vol. 1, 1956.
121. J.B.S. Haldane, 'The Argument from Animal to Men: an examination of its validity for

anthropology' in *Culture and the Evolution of Man*, (M.F. Ashley Montague ed), Oxford University Press, 1962.

122. W.H. Thorpe, 'The Language of Birds' *Scientific American* October, 1956.
123. Z.Y. Kuo, 'Further Study on the Behaviour of the Cat towards the Rat' *Journal of Comparative Psychology*, No. 25, 1938.
124. C.P. Haskins, *Of Ants and Men* George Allen and Unwin, London, 1974.
125. Gavin de Beer, *Embryos and Ancestors* Clarendon Press, Oxford, 1958.
126. Conrad Limbaugh, 'Cleaning Symbiosis' *Scientific American* August, 1961.
127. V.C. Wynne-Edwards, *Animal Disperson in Relation to Social Behaviour* Oliver and Boyd, Edinburgh/London, 1962.
128. Miriam Rothschild and Teresa Clay, *Fleas, Flukes and Cuckoos* Collins, London, 1952.
129. R.W.G. Hingston, *Problems of Instinct and Intelligence* Edward Arnold & Co., London, 1928.
130. George Peter Murdock, 'Anthropology as a comparative science' in *Culture and Society,* University of Pittsburgh Press, Pittsburgh, 1965.
131. George E. Simpson and David F. Aberle, 'Cultural deprivation and millenial movements: a discussion' in *Cultural and Social Anthropology* (P.B. Hammond, ed.) Macmillan, New York, 1964.
132. David F. Aberle, *The Peyote Religion among the Navaho* Aldine, Chicago, 1966.
133. Rafael Karsten, *La Civilisation de l'Empire Inca* Payot, Paris, 1957.
134. A.M. Vergiat, *Les Rites Secrets des Primitifs de L'Oubangui* Payot, Paris, 1936.
135. Robert R. Gray, 'Some parallels in Sonjo and Christian Mythology' in *African Systems of Thought* (M. Fortes and G. Dieterlen, eds.) Oxford University Press, Oxford, 1965.
136. Norman Cohn, *The Pursuit of the Millenium* Secker and Warburg, London, 1957.
137. Vittorio Lanternari, *Les Mouvements Religieux des Peuples Opprimés* Maspero, Paris, 1962.
138. Robert H. Lowie, 'Le Messianisme primitif: contribution a un probleme d'ethnologie' in *Diogene* No. 19, Gallimard, Paris, 1957.
139. This information was obtained by the author during a month spent on Mayotte and Grand Comore in February, 1968.
140. Bronislaw Malinowski, *The Dynamics of Cultural Change* Yale University Press, 1965.
141. Ibn Battuta, *Travels*.
142. Sir James Frazer, *The Golden Bough* Macmillan, London, 1923.
143. R.E. Bradbury, 'The Benin Kingdom and the Edo-speaking Peoples of South-Western Nigeria' in *Ethnographic Survey of Africa* — West African Part XII, International African Institute, London, 1957.
144. R.E. Bradbury, 'The Kingdom of Benin' in *West African Kingdom of the Nineteenth Century* (D. Forde and P. Kaberry eds.) Oxford University Press for the International African Institute, London, 1967.
145. R.E. Bradbury, 'The Social Structure of Benin, with Special Reference to the Politico-ritual Organisation' Unpublished PhD Thesis, University of London.
146. U.M. Lawal-Osula, (ed.) 'Benin Native Authority', *New Constitution*, 1948.
147. E.G. Parrinder, *West African Religions* 2nd Edition, London, 1961.
148. J.S. Mbiti, *Concepts of God in Africa* SPCK, London, 1970.
149. E.G. Parrinder, *African Traditional Religions* 2nd edition, London, 1962.
150. J.S. Mbiti, *African Religions and Philosophy* London and New York, 1969.
151. Robert L. Fantz, 'The Origin of Form Perception' in *Scientific American* May, 1962.
152. M|J. Harner, 'Jivaro Souls' *American Anthropologist* Vol. 64, No. 2, April 1966.
153. E.G.F. Sauer, 'Celestial Navigation of Birds' *Scientific American* August, 1958.
154. H.W. Lissman, 'Electric Location by Fishes' *Scientific American* March, 1963.
155. Ivo Kohler, 'Experiments with goggles' *Scientific American* May, 1962.
156. Konrad Lorenz, 'Gestalt perception as fundamental to scientific knowledge' *General Systems Yearbook* Vol. VII, 1962.
157. W.J. Wittreich 'Visual Perception and Personality' *Scientific American* April, 1959.
158. W. Ittleson and W. Kilpatrick, 'Experiments in perception' *Scientific American* August, 1951.
159. T.C.R. Bowen 'The Visual World of Infants' *Scientific American* December, 1961.
160. R. Melzac, 'The Perception of Pain' *Scientific American* February, 1968.
161. A.H. Riesen, 'Arrested Vision' *Scientific American* July, 1950.
162. J.A.L. Singh and Robert M. Zingg, *Wolf Children and Feral Man* Harper & Bros., New York, 1942.
163. H.F. Harlow and Margaret Kuenne, 'Learning to Think' *Scientific American* 1949.
164. S.E. Asch, 'Opinions & Social Pressure' *Scientific American* November 1955.
165. J.H. Woodger, *Biological Principles* Routledge and Kegan Paul, London, 1948.

166.   G. Wald, 'Innovation in Biology' *Scientific American* September, 1958.

167.   Gerald Feinberg, 'Ordinary Matter' *Scientific American* May, 1967.

168.   P.W. Bridgman, *The Logic of Modern Physics* Macmillan Co., New York, 1960.

# Index

*If you are interested in the 'Systems' or 'Ecological' approach to the problems our society faces today, you should subscribe to*

# The Ecologist

Journal of the Post Industrial Age

**THE ECOLOGIST**, the Journal of the Post-Industrial Age, was first published in 1970 and became famous through its world-renowned publication *A Blueprint for Survival*. In 1978 *The Ecologist* takes on a new look and generates two periodicals instead of one.

**THE NEW ECOLOGIST** will be published six times a year, keeping the present format. It will contain more topical material, more reports, more eco-politics, more critical analysis and more suggestions for practical solutions and contributions from people personally involved in all the different aspects of the struggle. It will remain serious, philosophical and committed to the ideal of an ecologically orientated post-industrial society.

**THE ECOLOGIST QUARTERLY** will continue to be the forum of thinkers who question the basic assumptions tht underlie conventional wisdom and who are trying to work out the philosophical, scientific and ideological foundations of the new societies that must eventually emerge from the debris of industrialism.

**IF YOU ARE NOT FAMILIAR WITH THE ECOLOGIST WHY NOT SEND FOR A FREE SAMPLE OF ONE OR BOTH OF OUR NEW PERIODICALS?**

**SUBSCRIPTION COUPON** (Block Capitals Please)

Name. . . . . . . . . . . . . . . . . . . . . . . . . . . Address. . . . . . . . . . . . . . . . . . . . . . . . . . . . . . . . . . . .

. . . . . . . . . . . . . . . . . . . . . . . . . . . . . . . . . . . . . . . . . . . . . . . . . . . . . . . . . . . . . . . . . . . . . . . . . . . . . . . . .

. . . . . . . . . . . . . . . . . . . . . . . . . . . . . . . . . . . . . . . . . . . . . . . . . . . . . . . . . . . . . . . . . . . . . . . . . . . . . . . . .

☐ I wish to subscribe to The New Ecologist for one year. I enclose cheque/money order etc. for £4.00 (US $9.00).

☐ I wish to subscribe to The Ecologist Quarterly for one year. I enclose cheque/money order etc. for £4.00 (US. $9.00).

☐ I wish to subscribe to both the above at the special combined rate of £7.00 (US. $16.00).

Please send me a free copy of The New Ecologist  ☐   The Quarterly Ecologist  ☐

Cheques and money orders should be crossed and made out to The Ecologist. Send this coupon to The Subscription Dept., The Ecologist, 73 Molesworth Street, Wadebridge, Cornwall, PL27 7DS, U.K.

*Note: Present subscribers will receive both publications until their current subs expire.*

Idle hands are the devil's workshop.